CMSRN Exam Prep 2020-2021

A Medical Surgical Nursing Study Guide with 450 Test Questions and Answers (3 Full Practice Tests - Med Surg Certification Review Book)

ISBN 978-1-989726-14-3 (papeback)
Published by Newstone Test Prep

Table of Contents

Introduction

The Certified Medical-Surgical Registered Nurse (CMSRN) certification program will help you enter the medical field. In order to receive your certification, you will be required to show that you comprehend, and are competent in, many aspects of medical care. Careful studying and a thorough understanding of what the exam is comprised of will help you to improve your chances of passing the test.

The following guide focuses on helping you prepare for the CMSRN exam. The guide thoroughly covers all six of the main domains that are tested on the exam. It also includes three separate tests of 150 questions each. These tests are designed to resemble the CMSRN test, so you get practice for the actual exam. In studying this book and taking the practice tests, you'll be able to identify your areas of weakness and strength.

This guide also discusses some of the most common mistakes people make on the CMSRN exam. By knowing ahead of time what the common errors are, you can better prepare yourself to avoid them.

Once you have passed the CMSRN, you will be qualified to enter the medical profession. As such, the exam is very important, and not to be taken lightly. This guide will help you thoroughly prepare to take the test.

Notice

All information is based on the standards that have been established by the Medical-Surgical Nursing Certification Board (MSNCB), the organization dedicated to confirming CMSRN candidates. Additional information on the CMSRN exam can be found at the official MSNCB website at msncb.org. This includes details on the specific places you can take the certification exam.

Chapter 1 – An Introduction To the Exam

The CMSRN exam is designed to test your understanding of how to care for patients. This requires in-depth knowledge, which this book will help you review. Additionally, in order to do well on the test you will need to be aware of how the exam is structured and how best to approach it on test day. This introduction focuses on what the CMSRN is and what it will do for your career.

What Is a CMSRN?

A CMSRN is a Certified Medical-Surgical Registered Nurse. This medical professional is capable of providing advanced nursing services to patients in various medical environments, including hospitals and places where patients are in need of complex surgeries.

Certification confirms a nurse's specialized knowledge. Someone who is CMSRN certified is expected to be able to identify the specific medical services and procedures that a patient may require. Additionally, a successful CMSRN must stay up to date on the latest innovations and procedures in the medical field.

In addition to serving as a professional badge that denotes advanced training, thereby garnering respect, CMSRN certification results in a higher earning potential.

Who Certifies CMSRN Professionals?

The CMSRN exam is administered by the Medical-Surgical Nursing Certification Board. The organization is affiliated with the Academy of Medical-Surgical Nurses. You can learn more about the MSNCB by visiting msncb.org.

Are You Eligible To Complete the Exam?

In order to be eligible to take the CMSRN exam, you must:

1. Have a current license as a registered nurse, valid in the United States, any American territory or Canada.
2. Have practiced as a registered nurse in a medical-surgical environment for at least two full years.
3. Have attained at least 2,000 hours of practice in the last three years in a medical-surgical environment. These hours could include clinical rotations, education or management work.

Exam Specifics

The CMSRN exam is three hours long. It involves 150 questions and is administered by computer.

The questions on the test are arranged in order of domain. Refer to the Domains and Content Areas section of this guide to review the specific sections of the test.

During the exam, you have the opportunity to return to any answers that you might be uncertain about. Throughout the exam, you can always come back to any question and change your answer.

Test Locations and Scheduling the Exam

You can complete the exam at a Prometric test site. Visit prometric.com to find information on the testing site nearest to you. Be aware that not all Prometric test sites administer the CMSRN exam.

Before you can schedule a testing time, you need an Authorization To Test (ATT). The ATT will be provided to you by the MSNCB after your application has been reviewed and accepted. You should receive the ATT within a week, although it may even arrive the same day you apply to take the test, depending on how many applications were submitted before yours. After you receive the ATT, you have a 90-day period during which you can schedule your exam.

The CMSRN exam is scheduled on a first-come, first-serve basis. Because of this, it is advisable to schedule your exam as early as possible during that 90-day window.

In order to take the exam, you'll need to report to your assigned testing center. You'll be asked to provide a valid government-issued photo identification card with you. This can be a driver's license, passport or any other government-issued identification with your picture on it. It's best if your identification has your signature.

Exam Fees

The CMSRN exam application fee is $375. This includes a nonrefundable processing and administration fee of $75. Members of the Academy of Medical-Surgical Nurses (AMSN) pay a reduced fee of $255.

How Is the Exam Scored?

You need a score of at least 95 to pass. This requires you to answer about 71 percent of the test questions correctly.

You will also receive sub-scores for each of the individual domains. You can use these sub-scores to get an idea of areas you need to improve, whether it's to study to retake the exam after failing it, or in order to prepare to take the test again when it's time to renew your certification.

Be aware that while the test has 150 questions, only 125 are scored. The other questions help the MSNCB improve future versions of the exam.

You will receive your score immediately after finishing the exam. You can also get the scores sent to you by email within 24 hours of taking the test.

Statistically speaking, the potential for you to succeed on the CMSRN exam is high. According to the MSNCB, about 7,000 people were tested in 2018. Approximately 81 percent of those people passed the exam, while about 2,500 more received their recertification. In all, as of 2018, there were more than 34,000 CMSRNs active in the field.

What If You Fail?

You have the option to retake the CMSRN exam if you fail. You'll be required to wait one week after taking the test before applying to retake the exam, and then you'll have a 90-day window during which to schedule your retake. That retake is required to be a minimum of four months from the original exam date.

The first-time retake fee is $300, or $180 for AMSN members. If you retake the test three times, the fee will be $375, like the first time you took the test.

If you've failed the exam and are retaking it, it's critical to review the sub-scores from your test. These will help you identify strengths and weaknesses and will help guide your studies so you do better on the next exam attempt.

Recertification

CMSRN certification is good for five years. After that, you'll need to apply for recertification.

This recertification process is to ensure that CMSRNs remain up to date on the newest developments in the medical and nursing fields. This includes being aware of how the industry is changing and being able to demonstrate knowledge gained during years of practice in the field.

There are two ways to apply for recertification:

1. By continuing your education

Continuing education programs where you have had at least 90 contact hours and 1,000 practice hours in a medical-surgical setting in the last five years are considered an acceptable form of recertification.

2. By exam

If you have had at least 2,000 practice hours in a medical-surgical setting in the last three years, you can take the CMSRN exam again in order to be recertified. These hours include practice in a clinical setting, educational setting or management setting. You must have practiced for at least two years as a registered nurse in that setting.

You must apply for recertification at least 30 days before your current certification expires. This is to ensure that there are no CMSRNs in the field who are working under a lapsed certification.

Chapter 2 – The Domains and Content Areas of the CMSRN Exam

The CMSRN exam covers various aspects of the medical field. The more you know about the content of the test, the better you can prepare yourself to successfully take it.

The 150 questions are divided between two separate domains, with six or seven content areas in each domain. The following chart shows how the MSNCB has structured the CMSRN exam as of January 2019:

Type of Patient Problem	Average Number of Questions
Gastrointestinal	25
Pulmonary	25
Cardiovascular	25
Diabetes	25
Urological	25
Musculoskeletal	25
Total	**150**

Patient Problems

Exam questions are divided up based on six different patient problems. You will have to identify matters pertaining to the body's main systems and how they directly impact patients' health. You'll need to know what can impact the body's systems and be well versed in how to respond appropriately. Your knowledge of medical and surgical procedures will be tested.

The test sections in this part of the exam are:

1. Gastrointestinal

The gastrointestinal (GI) system refers to the tract where a person takes in food, digests its contents and absorbs its nutrients and energy. The system also expels waste. This test section focuses on all the parts of the GI system, including the mouth, esophagus, intestines and stomach.

2. Pulmonary

The pulmonary system focuses on the body's ability to efficiently take in oxygen and expel it as carbon dioxide. The lungs and other related parts of the body are also covered in this test section.

3. Cardiovascular/Hematological

The cardiovascular and hematological segment of the exam focuses on the blood, heart, veins, arteries and other parts of the cardiovascular system. Your knowledge of heart disease and other cardiovascular-related failures will be tested.

The hematological section of the test concentrates on the function of blood within the human body. You'll also be tested on immunological concerns. Other organs such as the bone marrow, spleen, skin, lymph nodes, hair, nails, endocrine glands and other bodily organs that directly relate to blood formation and functionality may also be discussed. This test section could include topics such as psoriasis, HIV/AIDS and various forms of hepatitis.

4. Diabetes/Endocrine/Immunological

This section of the test focuses on type 1 and type 2 diabetes.

The endocrine system involves glands that regulate the body's metabolic functions, growth, tissue functionality, sexual actions and reproduction, sleep and mood. You'll be tested on the glands' functions and disorders.

The immunological system helps the body prevent infections or fight them once they've been contracted. The lymph nodes, thymus, appendix and other aspects of the immune system are critical to this part of the test.

5. Urological/Renal

The urological system involves the kidneys, bladder, urethra, prostate and other functions devoted to the processing of liquid waste. The renal system directly links to this segment and focuses on removing the waste that is processed.

6. Musculoskeletal/Neurological/Integumentary

The musculoskeletal system is critical to the support and motion of the body, including muscles, tendons, cartilage and joints. The neurological system focuses on the brain and other parts of the body that help to transmit signals that regulate certain body functions. The integumentary system focuses on the hair, nails, skin and other external organs.

(Note: The CMSRN exam used to have seven patient problems, with one segment devoted to hematological, immunological and integumentary issues. That segment has been absorbed into other sections of the exam, as noted above.)

Domains of Practice

Seven separate domains of practice are tested on the exam:

1. Helping Role

Your ability to help patients is critical to the success of your work. This part of the exam concentrates on your ability to provide patients with the assistance they require. You will be tested on your ability to assess a patient's level of comfort or pain. You'll also be tested on whether you know how to appropriately adjust treatments and services based on a patient's comfort level. Part of this includes knowing when to provide pharmacological intervention and when to administer a treatment that doesn't require drug use.

This part of the test assesses your understanding of many aspects pertaining to a patient's unique needs. This includes important considerations such as cultural preferences.

End-of-life care considerations are also covered on this part of the test. This includes pain management and other end-of-life issues such as recognizing the decisions a patient or the patient's family makes regarding treatment, and dealing with those decisions appropriately.

2. Teaching and Coaching

The teaching and coaching segment of the exam assesses your ability to educate your patients. As a CMSRN, you'll need to be able to teach your patient and/or that patient's loved ones how best to care for him/herself. You will need to be able to assess how well a patient is capable of learning, any barriers he or she has to learning and be informed about the most appropriate resources you can provide to help further address a patient's specific needs.

3. Diagnostic and Patient Monitoring

This section is one of the more important ones on the test, as denoted by the larger number of questions in the segment. You will be tested on how well you monitor patients, collect data and create an appropriate treatment plan. Additionally, you'll be tested on your ability to assess a patient's health condition.

There may be times when deviations in the treatment process occur. These include cases where a patient is not responding to a treatment as well as expected. A CMSRN's ability to observe and document such changes is critical to a patient's health. Information on how to identify concerns that might influence how well a patient responds to treatments will also be covered.

4. Administering Treatments/Nursing Interventions

This domain is extremely important and contains a large number of questions. You'll be tested on how to administer medications, how to identify how well a treatment is working and how to identify various symptoms and other signs of concern. The use of adaptive or assistive devices will also be discussed, based on how they support a patient's mobility or comfort.

5. Managing Emergencies

Situations in the nursing field can change at any moment. This part of the exam covers how effectively you manage an emergency. You'll be tested on how you manage changes and take specific actions based upon individual emergency situations. You'll also be tested on basic life support skills.

Emergencies such as chest pains, a heart attack or stroke will be included in this section. This subsection of the exam will help you understand what you need to do if you encounter any of these medical crises.

6. Ensuring Quality

This segment of the exam is fairly short and is generally considered the least important part of the test. However, the few questions are critical to conveying your ability to work with other people in a medical environment. The quality aspect focuses on how you collect and report data pertaining to failures. The ability to move orders between parties and effectively communicate with everyone is critical.

7. Role Competency

This is the second-least essential part of the exam. It assesses how you prioritize work, delegate tasks and identify the roles of the individual healthcare members that you are expected to work with. You'll be expected to be able to create a work plan that includes how many people are involved and how many tasks will be required to complete the assignment.

Chapter 3 – Gastrointestinal Health

The gastrointestinal system refers to the digestive system. The stomach, intestines, liver, pancreas and other parts of the GI system are critical for practicing nurses to have a thorough knowledge and understanding of.

Gastrointestinal Bleeding

Bleeding can develop in the upper or lower part of the GI system. A Mallory-Weiss tear is a potential concern, although GI bleeding is more often a sign of various cancers.

A person who uses nonsteroidal anti-inflammatory drugs (NSAIDs) is at an elevated risk of experiencing GI bleeding. Individuals who experience gastroesophageal reflux disorder (GERD) are also at a higher risk.

A patient can experience various forms of discomfort pertaining to GI bleeding, including abdominal discomfort. Individuals may notice bright red, bloody stools, though this is not always the case. It's important to note that GI bleeding isn't always visible to a patient.

An endoscope may be introduced into the GI system in order to identify where the bleeding is located. A complete blood count test may also be useful in diagnosing the problem.

Medical treatment for GI bleeding is heavily dependent on identifying the reason for the condition. Proper fluid replacement is critical. Temporary use of isotonic crystalloids may be necessary. However, the use of the crystalloids is not a substitute for promptly locating and treating the source of the bleeding.

Cirrhosis

Cirrhosis occurs when scar tissue develops in the liver, replacing the live, healthy cells. Lipids are likely to be stored in the body's cells due to cirrhosis, thereby reducing the liver's ability to function correctly.

Abdominal pain, drowsiness and unexplained weight loss are common signs of cirrhosis. Patients who have hepatitis C are at an elevated risk of developing the condition.

Antiviral agents can be prescribed, especially in the case of a patient who has hepatitis C. Diuretics and beta-blockers may also help if the cirrhosis begins to influence the heart's overall functionality.

Zinc supplementation is strongly recommended for individuals with cirrhosis as the body's natural zinc levels may be depleted due to the condition.

A liver transplant is recommended in situations where the cirrhosis has become so extensive that the liver is no longer able to function due to scarring.

Foreign Bodies

A foreign body can become lodged in the GI system when someone accidentally swallows something inedible, such as a small child who puts a tiny toy in his or her mouth. Many objects can become stuck in the oropharynx. In some cases, a foreign body will move through the esophagus and into the stomach, where it may be expelled through the body's digestive system. However, some foreign bodies can become stuck in the small intestine. Items that are two centimeters big or longer could cause an intestinal blockage.

Logically, small children are at the highest risk of foreign bodies in the GI tract. Patients who have dentures may also be at a higher risk. Psychiatric patients who may not be thinking clearly also have higher risk factors as they may consume inedible objects.

An X-ray can identify an intestinal blockage. An ultrasound is recommended if the blockage appears to be due to a sharp object that could cause serious harm if not quickly removed.

Treatment of a foreign body depends on the type and size of the object. Promotility medications may be used in cases where an item is deemed safe to move through the intestines and can be excreted naturally without causing any damage. A laparoscopic procedure is required when the object in question is overly large, sharp, toxic or can cause other types of damage.

GI Obstructions

A GI obstruction should not be confused with a foreign body as an obstruction is made up of the body's own tissues.

An endoscopy may identify a possible obstruction and can help physicians determine the best way to safely remove it. Antibiotic treatments may also help with resolving the situation. A colectomy may also be required. Bowel rest may also be prescribed, to ease the stress on a patient's intestines.

Surgical intervention is not necessary for an obstruction unless the situation worsens and potentially puts the patient's health at risk. If a patient begins to hemorrhage, surgery is immediately required.

Gastroenteritis

Gastroenteritis develops when the GI system is irritated, potentially due to norovirus. Various bacteria may trigger the issue, such as if a person drinks contaminated water or eats tainted food. A foreign body may also cause gastroenteritis.

The condition can trigger diarrhea, nausea and vomiting. As a result, fluid replacement is recommended for a patient. A person might experience an elevated heart rate or unanticipated weight loss.

Antibiotics may be used in some cases. Antidiarrheal medication may also help control the issue and lessen fluid loss. The condition may be self-resolving at times, so treatment must be based on careful monitoring to determine what a patient does and does not need in the way of intervention.

Inflammatory Issues

Inflammatory Bowel Disease

Inflammatory bowel disease (IBD) is a condition where the GI system responds negatively to bacteria naturally found in the intestine. This irritates the GI tract and can cause varying levels of harm, depending on the severity of the condition.

Crohn's Disease

Crohn's disease is a type of IBD that occurs in the small intestine. The severity of the condition will vary by patient.

Crohn's disease can cause abdominal pain and cramping, as well as diarrhea. Blood may appear in the stool. A person may also experience a reduced appetite and weight loss.

When a patient presents with Crohn's disease, a blood test is recommended for identifying anemia or to rule out an infection. A fecal occult blood test may also be used to identify any blood in the stool.

A colonoscopy may help with identifying existing damage to the intestine. It may also help identify granulomas, a series of inflammatory cells that can trigger the effects of Crohn's disease.

Anti-inflammatory drugs can help with controlling the symptoms of Crohn's. Corticosteroids may help, although the effectiveness will vary based on the condition. Oral 5-aminosalicylates are also necessary for controlling the condition.

There is no cure for Crohn's disease. Patients will require lifelong treatment to manage their symptoms in order to be able to live life as comfortably as possible.

Ulcerative Colitis

Ulcerative colitis causes inflammation and ulcers or sores within the digestive tract including the lining of the large intestine and the rectum.

Diarrhea is a common symptom among people with ulcerative colitis. The diarrhea may contain blood or pus, depending on the extent of the condition.

Abdominal pains or rectal bleeding will occur among many patients with ulcerative colitis. A person may also experience an urgent need to defecate.

The type of ulcerative colitis varies based on the area that the condition has developed in:

1. Proctosigmoiditis causes inflammation in the rectum and sigmoid colon, along with blood diarrhea.
2. Left-sided colitis appears from the sigmoid and descending colon.
3. Pancolitis influences the entire colon.

Antibiotics and corticosteroids may be effective treatments. The key is to ensure that there are no recurring attacks. Given that the condition has no cure, patients must be treated for ulcerative colitis to prevent recurrences (flare-ups) as much as possible.

Cholecystitis

Cholecystitis is an inflammation of the gallbladder due to a cystic duct blockage caused by gallstones.

Older individuals and females are at an elevated risk of contracting cholecystitis. People who are overweight or have experienced a significant amount of weight loss are also a higher risk for the condition.

Symptoms include pain in the right upper quadrant along with vomiting, nausea, jaundice and fever. The area around the gallbladder may be tender. There is a potential for the organ to become infected if not treated, thus leading to gangrene.

A liver function test may be necessary to ensure a correct diagnosis. An ultrasound can also be performed to help confirm the condition. The ultrasound is ideal for women who need confirmation as to whether their condition is related to cholecystitis or pregnancy.

Antibiotic treatments may be required. For the most severe cases, a cholecystectomy will be required. It's vital that cholecystitis be treated as soon as possible to prevent worsening symptoms.

Gastritis

Gastritis is an inflammation in the stomach lining. The condition is usually accompanied by abdominal pain, nausea and vomiting.

The use of corticosteroids or NSAIDs may trigger the condition. People who consume excessive amounts of alcohol are also more likely to experience gastritis due to GI irritation.

Gastritis can be treated through antibiotics and antacids, although the effectiveness of the medications may vary based on the severity of the condition. Antidiarrheal medication may also be effective in helping to control the condition.

Appendicitis

Appendicitis is a condition where the appendix becomes inflamed. The organ becomes blocked by fecaliths or parasites, among other bacteria, and swells accordingly. If the appendix ruptures before it is removed, peritonitis and sepsis may occur, followed by death.

A patient may experience sharp pains in the right lower quadrant. A loss of appetite and/or vomiting are other possible symptoms of the condition.

An ultrasound may help identify the inflamed appendix. For women, a pregnancy test should be performed to confirm that the condition is appendicitis and not an undetected pregnancy.

Antibiotic treatment is recommended. An appendectomy, meaning the surgical removal of the appendix, is required in cases where the appendix has ruptured or is not responding to standard treatment.

Diverticulitis

Diverticulitis is an inflammation that causes pouches or sacs (diverticula) to form in the wall of the large intestine. The condition is more common among people 50 years of age or older.

Exerting undue pressure during defecation, thereby irritating the bowels, can trigger diverticulitis. Debris can fill the diverticula, causing inflammation and substantial pain in the lower left quadrant. Vomiting, fever and chills may also occur.

Antibiotic treatment is required for the condition. IV fluids are encouraged. Bowel rest, by way of a low-fiber diet or a clear liquid diet until the symptoms start to disappear, may be prescribed. A high-fiber diet may eventually start to control the condition, although that will depend on the individual patient.

The level of inflammation will dictate further treatment. A colectomy may be necessary in the most severe cases. This involves resecting the damaged part of the intestine with a healthier segment, essentially redirecting the bowel and removing the diverticula.

Peritonitis

Peritonitis is an inflammation in the peritoneum, a serosal membrane in the abdominal cavity.

The peritoneum can become infected due to a pathogen or ruptured appendix. Bile from a punctured gallbladder or liver may also enter the cavity and cause irritation.

The condition may trigger abdominal pains, nausea, vomiting, diarrhea, fever, chills and abdominal distension.

A blood test or X-ray of the abdomen may help identify the condition. If not treated promptly, peritonitis may become a recurring problem.

Treatment involves resolving the infection or the source of the concern. Antibiotic therapy is strongly encouraged to prevent the problem from spreading to other parts of the body.

Esophagitis

Esophagitis is the inflammation of the lining inside the esophagus. The issue may be caused by candida or another infectious agent, GERD, HIV, herpes or various forms of chemotherapy.

A patient suffering from esophagitis may experience recurring nausea, hoarseness or sepsis. A patient may also experience a surprising amount of weight loss. In the worst cases, perforation of the esophagus may develop.

A complete blood count test is recommended to identify any unusual changes in natural hemoglobin and hematocrit levels. An endoscopy or an ECG may help to confirm that the pain is related to esophagitis and is not a cardiac-related issue.

Since GERD may be a contributing factor to esophagitis, lifestyle changes may be necessary to prevent GERD from developing. Blood component replacement may also be required in some of the more significant cases. If additional treatment is required, corticosteroids may be prescribed for a limited time.

If the esophagus is perforated, surgery may be required.

Hernia

A hernia occurs when a portion of the bowel is displaced and an organ or fatty tissue then pushes through the weakened muscle.

A hernia may be triggered by an injury, a surgical procedure or another kind of medical intervention.

In some cases, the hernia may have a substantial impact on the blood flow in the area. If this occurs, the hernia may not be able to be repaired.

Some hernias visibly protrude, although even 'invisible' hernias may cause intense pain. That pain may radiate to other parts of the body.

A CT scan is required in order to confirm the presence of a hernia. A flat-plate review can also be used to identify the air that is released due to the bowel perforation.

In most cases, the hernia will heal on its own with regular care. Such care may include instructing the patient to avoid lifting or straining. To prevent constipation, which leads to bowel straining and can contribute to the worsening of the hernia, a high-fiber diet may also be prescribed.

Emergency surgery is required for hernias that may become irreversible. During the surgery, the affected bowel segment is resected in order to restore blood flow to the target area. This process restores bowel functionality and helps to prevent perforation or GI blockages.

Hepatitis

Hepatitis is an inflammation in the liver usually caused by a virus that is transmitted through fecal contact, sexual activity or perinatal transmission.

There are five types of hepatitis:

1. Hepatitis A – The condition is triggered by the consumption of water or food that has been contaminated by the fecal matter of a person with the virus.

2. Hepatitis B – The virus is transmitted by contact with the bodily fluids of a person with the virus. People may also contract hepatitis B through sex with an infected partner or by sharing drug needles or razors.

3. Hepatitis C – The virus is transmitted through contact with the bodily fluids of an infected person, usually via drug use or sex.

4. Hepatitis D – The hepatitis B virus can evolve over time and become hepatitis D.

5. Hepatitis E – Hepatitis E occurs in cases where a person comes into contact with dirty or contaminated water. This type of hepatitis is more likely to develop in Central America, Africa and other parts of the world where sanitation is lacking.

Hepatitis can be contracted through contact with others who are infected, although some noninfectious cases of the condition exist. For example, a person who consumes excess alcohol quantities may be at risk of the disease. The condition can harm the liver and possibly cause inflammation. Diseases or lifestyles that cause scarring to the liver may lead to hepatitis.

An autoimmune response may also trigger the condition. The immune system might identify a foreign body within the liver and start to attack the organ. This then damages the liver and causes hepatitis, though the type and severity depend on the damage.

Symptoms of hepatitis include fatigue and flu-like signs. A person may also develop dark urine and light-colored stools. Abdominal pain and a general loss of appetite may also occur. Jaundice, a condition where the skin and eyes become yellow, may also develop in some patients. The symptoms will progress gradually, so there is a potential for a patient to be ill with hepatitis for a while without being aware of it, thereby infecting others.

Bleeding, ascites or kidney failure occur in the most severe cases of diabetes.

Hepatitis may be diagnosed through a physical exam. The abdomen is palpated for any tenderness. A sonogram or other exam may be used to identify whether the liver is enlarged. Jaundice is also a clue physicians will take note of when making a diagnosis.

A blood test to assess liver function and identify any viruses may be administered. Additionally, a biopsy may also be required to identify if there is a significant infection.

Treatment will vary based on the type of hepatitis. The treatment options include:

1. Hepatitis A – Hepatitis A doesn't last long and doesn't require any specific medical treatment, although bed rest and proper hydration are recommended. The hepatitis A vaccination is recommended for toddlers, although the vaccination can work for adults as well.

2. Hepatitis B – Antiviral medications can help. Newborns should receive the hepatitis B vaccine. The time frame for how long it will take a person with hepatitis B to heal will depend on the severity of the condition.

3. Hepatitis C – Antiviral medications may help in the treatment of hepatitis C. A person who has severe liver damage due to hepatitis C may potentially require a liver transplant.

4. Hepatitis D – There are no antiviral treatments for hepatitis D. Given that hepatitis B may become hepatitis D, infants are given a hepatitis B vaccine in order to prevent the condition.

5. Hepatitis E – The condition may resolve on its own, although it is best for the patient to get enough rest and to stay well hydrated. Pregnant women who contract hepatitis E will require special monitoring to ensure the health of both the mother and the fetus.

Patients should be encouraged to avoid sharing razors, needles and other things with people who have hepatitis. It also helps to avoid drinking water and eating raw foods when visiting developing countries.

Patients with hepatitis must avoid consuming alcohol as this directly impacts the liver and can therefore worsen the condition.

Esophageal Varices

Esophageal varices, which are swollen veins in the lining of the esophagus, occur when hypertension (high blood pressure) develops in the liver. Due to the condition, blood may not circulate freely into the liver because the blood vessels are constricted. Because of the high pressure they're under, there's a chance of blood vessels rupturing or the liver being damaged.

A patient who regularly experiences constipation may require additional medical intervention to prevent varices. Alcoholics are more prone to esophageal varices because of their overconsumption of alcohol, which affects the liver.

Prophylactics may be administered in cases where the varices are five millimeters or larger in diameter. Cases where red streaks appear along the varices require prophylactics.

A person who has esophageal varices will be at an elevated risk of developing a hemorrhage. An endoscopy should be performed in order to correctly diagnose the condition. The process involves lightening the varices and/or inserting a shunt. Colloid and crystalloid fluid replacement may also be recommended.

Intussusception

Intussusception involves part of an intestine slipping into another part of the bowel, thereby causing a blockage. The condition, which is fatal if not swiftly treated, is more likely to develop among infants.

The issue may be preceded by an upper respiratory infection. Vomiting and intense abdominal pain can cause intussusception and therefore should be carefully monitored and treated. Diarrhea that contains mucus and blood can be a common sign of the condition.

A contrast enema may identify an intussusception. A barium enema may help treat the condition. If the barium enema is unsuccessful, surgery will be necessary to resect the damaged part of the bowel.

Pancreatitis

Pancreatitis is the inflammation of the pancreas. The condition appears quickly and results in diarrhea, vomiting and significant abdominal pain. Abdominal distension may also occur in some patients.

The pancreas typically secretes enzymes necessary for digestive processes. When pancreatitis occurs, the pancreas is unable to perform its usual exocrine function, thereby causing the pancreas to secrete an excess of hormones. The elevated enzyme level produces an inflammatory response.

Excess alcohol consumption may be a contributing factor to pancreatitis. Edema may occur in some patients, along with necrosis of the pancreas in the most severe forms of the condition.

A P-amylase test is necessary to confirm the condition. Additional imaging exams can help to ascertain its severity.

Fluids may be administered intravenously to prevent the condition from worsening. Patients should be prescribed bowel rest.

Surgery may be necessary to remove damaged tissue and repair the pancreatic duct.

Peptic Ulcer

An ulcer can develop in the stomach, where it becomes a peptic (digestive or gastric) ulcer. The sore first appears on the lining in the stomach, and then it may move to the small intestine or esophagus.

A duodenal ulcer develops in the upper part of the small intestine, known as the duodenum.

A patient with a peptic ulcer will feel intense stomach pain. A general feeling of fullness or bloating may also occur, whether or not the patient has recently consumed a meal. Heartburn and nausea may also develop. Severe symptoms include vomiting (which may or may not include blood), dark blood in the stool, breathing difficulties and a general feeling of weakness.

The peptic ulcer may be triggered by a bacterium. Regular aspirin use or the use of other pain relievers may be a contributing factor to the ulcer's development. Additionally, steroids, anticoagulants and SSRIs may elevate the risk of contracting the condition. In particular, people who smoke or regularly consume alcohol may be at an elevated risk of developing ulcers.

An endoscopy or barium swallow may be used to identify the ulcer. The barium swallow coats the digestive system, thus making it easier to visually examine. Additionally, an X-ray may be helpful in locating the precise place where the ulcer has developed.

Antibiotic medications are used in treating a peptic ulcer. Additionally, medications such as proton-pump inhibitors can assist in blocking the production of acid while supporting the body's natural healing process. Antacids may also be used to neutralize the effect of stomach acid, although they should be used as a supplemental treatment as they will not heal the ulcer on their own. Some ulcers may be antibiotic-resistant.

Surgery should not be required for a peptic ulcer as a non-surgical treatment for peptic ulcers is both effective and viable. However, an ulcer that refuses to heal or which becomes life-threatening will require surgical intervention, possibly via endoscopy.

Patients with peptic ulcers should avoid using tobacco, alcohol, frequent NSAIDs, aspirin and other painkillers.

GI Trauma

A patient may experience gastrointestinal trauma for many reasons including excess physical force exerted upon the abdomen, often from a car wreck. Other types of GI trauma include penetration from a stabbing, gunshot or other item that directly enters the body.

GI trauma may cause hemorrhaging in the digestive tract. Depending on the severity of the injury, tachycardia or hypotension may also occur.

Any trauma-related event requires a full patient history in order to learn how the injury occurred and determine treatment.

A CT scan may help to confirm the extent of the damage. It could potentially reveal additional injuries that have not yet presented themselves symptomatically.

Chapter 4 – Pulmonary Health

The pulmonary system is also known as the respiratory system. It includes the lungs and airways. As such, all aspects pertaining to breathing are tested in this segment of the exam.

Types of Aspiration

Aspiration refers to when materials enter the pulmonary system. These include foreign compounds that could potentially be harmful, whether large foreign bodies or small particles.

Pneumonia

Pneumonia is an infection in the lungs triggered by inflammation in the air sacs (alveoli). The condition may be triggered by lung cancer, exposure to a parasite or a bacterial infection such as streptococcus and mycoplasma.

In some cases, pneumonia may be contracted based on specific circumstances. Aspiration pneumonia occurs when a patient inhales something contaminated. Nosocomial pneumonia develops within a hospital setting and may occur if a person has been hospitalized with another condition for at least 48 hours. Community-acquired pneumonia is more common as it is not contracted while in a hospital setting but while out and about among other people who may have the contagious infection.

A chest X-ray may be used to pinpoint the location, which may vary. A lobar infection will appear on one lobe of the lungs. Bronchopneumonia may occur if the infection appears throughout the lungs. An interstitial infection occurs in areas located between the alveoli.

A patient with pneumonia will experience a fever, dyspnea, chest pains and a cough. The cough may be "dry," and not produce anything such as mucus, especially if the mycoplasma bacterium is involved. The fever may or may not include chills.

A chest X-ray or a complete blood count with a differential review is recommended. A CT scan can also be performed if lung cancer is considered to be a possibility.

Antibiotic treatment is recommended for patients with pneumonia, although the type will vary based on the type of pneumonia. For streptococcus-based pneumonia, moxifloxacin or levofloxacin are recommended. For mycoplasma-based forms, clarithromycin and erythromycin are best.

CA-MRSA Pneumonia

Community-acquired methicillin-resistant staphylococcus aureus (CA-MRSA) pneumonia occurs in hospital-based pneumonia cases. Most people who contract CA-MRSA are first hospitalized for influenza. The condition must be rapidly diagnosed and treated, as it is fatal if allowed to advance.

A chest X-ray may be used to help confirm the condition. Linezolid may be used if the patient does not respond to the initial treatment.

Aspiration Pneumonitis

Aspiration pneumonitis results when foreign substances enter the lungs upon swallowing. This includes food, drinks or other compounds. While the epiglottis is responsible for preventing aspiration, the cartilage may fail to do its job. A bacterial infection may develop in the pulmonary system as a result of aspiration.

People who have experienced GERD, multiple sclerosis, head trauma or consumed alcohol or drugs are more likely to develop aspiration pneumonia.

A person with aspiration pneumonitis may present with a fever, dyspnea, tachypnea, hypotension, chest pains or cyanosis. A patient may also experience a full airway obstruction.

The most significant symptoms of aspiration pneumonia occur within 24 to 48 hours after the foreign body is inhaled.

A chest X-ray may help determine the severity of the condition. A complete blood count may also help; a high white blood cell count is one potential sign of infection.

The upper airway may need to be suctioned to remove the foreign substances which caused the pneumonia. Oxygen supplementation is required as part of standard treatment. Mechanical ventilation helps if there is a more significant concern.

Antibiotics may be prescribed for aspiration pneumonia that has lasted 24 to 48 hours after other standard treatment.

Foreign Body Aspiration

Foreign body aspiration occurs when an object becomes lodged in the larynx or trachea. This is an emergency situation due to the potential for the patient to suffocate.

The foreign body may be anything, including small bits of food. The right lung is more likely to be influenced by the foreign body, as the right mainstem bronchus directly leads to the lungs due to the positioning and angle.

A person may develop intense coughing, wheezing, choking and/or chest pains.

A CT scan or X-ray may identify the location of the foreign body.

In cases where acute choking occurs, the Heimlich maneuver is recommended. If a patient is not choking, a bronchoscopy may be indicated, whether rigid or flexible as appropriate. A surgical bronchoscopy is only necessary in cases where traditional treatment is not working.

Secondary pneumonia may develop after the foreign body is removed and may be treated with antibiotics. Oxygen supplementation may also be used to assist the patient.

Viral Pneumonia

Viral pneumonia is an infection of the airway that develops primarily among children and the elderly, due to their weakened immune systems. The influenza virus is a common concern.

Symptoms may include a nonproductive cough, a fever or chills, fatigue, headache, wheezing and cyanosis.

A chest X-ray may be used to view the lungs and thereby identify the condition. A viral culture may also be taken, although results may take a few weeks and therefore this should not be the sole method of diagnosis.

Antiviral medications may be used in the treatment of viral pneumonia. Oseltamivir or zanamivir may help.

Supplemental oxygen may assist a patient in recovery, along with intravenous fluids. Bed rest should be encouraged. Mechanical ventilation is only necessary for the most severe cases of viral pneumonia.

COPD

Chronic obstructive pulmonary disease (COPD) is a condition where airflow is blocked in the lungs, thus making it difficult for the patient to breathe. The condition may include two distinct problems:

1. Bronchitis – Mucus develops, and the airways become inflamed.
2. Emphysema – Air spaces around the airways are damaged. Some spaces may become enlarged and therefore make it difficult to allow the passage of air.

Asthma is not the same thing as COPD, though people with COPD may develop asthma.

COPD can produce wheezing and coughing, fatigue, a fever, chest tightness and changes in breathing and exercise habits.

A chest X-ray or CT scan may be used to examine the lungs. Pulmonary function tests may also be performed to assess the force vital capacity. A total under 60 percent is a concern.

Oxygen supplementation may assist a patient, along with beta-2 agonists, antibiotics and corticosteroids.

Bronchitis

Bronchitis is the inflammation of the bronchial tubes that go from the trachea to the lungs. The influenza, streptococcus pneumoniae and chlamydia viruses may cause bronchitis. Exposure to smoke and pollution may further aggravate the condition once it has already been contracted.

A patient with pneumonia will present with an intense cough. It may be difficult or painful for a person to speak. Breathing may be quieter than normal as a patient may be trying to be careful, in order to avoid pain.

A complete blood count may be performed with a differential analysis to assess how the patient is responding. An elevated white blood cell count may indicate an infection. A chest X-ray may also be performed to determine the severity of the condition.

Bronchitis typically goes away in a few days. Bed rest is usually prescribed, sometimes along with Beta2-agonists to control coughing. NSAIDs may also be prescribed to relieve pain. Bronchitis is contagious and can be passed through respiratory droplets such as when a person coughs or sneezes. Therefore, a patient should wear a face mask and/or avoid speaking to prevent transmitting the infection.

If bronchitis refuses to resolve and might trigger a more significant medical concern, it may require treatment with antibiotics. Such medications are ideal for elderly patients who may have other underlying conditions which the bronchitis could exacerbate.

Bronchiolitis

Bronchiolitis is an inflammation in the airways within the lungs or the bronchioles. The condition occurs mainly in younger children, particularly those under two years of age.

Bronchiolitis spreads through direct contact with various respiratory droplets.

Symptoms may include fever, congestion, coughing, hypoxia, apnea and tachycardia. A child may also have difficulty eating, depending on the severity of the condition.

A white blood cell test or C-reactive protein test may be used to diagnose the condition.

Bronchiolitis will resolve itself in a week or two. Oxygen supplementation may be provided, although this is not always necessary. Patients should be kept consistently hydrated.

Croup

Acute laryngotracheobronchitis, more commonly referred to as croup, is an inflammation that develops in the trachea, larynx and bronchi.

Children under age six are more likely to develop croup.

The most prominent symptom of croup is a high-pitched or barking sound when breathing, suggesting that the airways are partially obstructed. Cyanosis, hypoxemia and respiratory failure may develop in some patients.

A chest X-ray should be performed on the glottis to assess whether the airway is narrowed.

Corticosteroids may be prescribed. Ventilation may be used in the most severe or significant cases where a patient is struggling to breathe. Although cool misting may also help, it is not necessarily as popular as it used to be, nor is it believed to be as effective as was once thought.

Any cases where an adult develops croup may be signs of an allergic reaction or other health threat.

Asthma

Asthma is a condition where a person's airways become inflamed and narrowed, potentially producing mucus, which makes breathing difficult.

Asthma can develop in people of all ages. It is more likely to be noticed in children, but adults are also frequently diagnosed with the condition.

The intensity of asthma will vary based on the patient. Some symptoms may be treated through the use of a bronchodilator to relieve breathing issues and to open airways. In other cases, status asthmaticus can develop if the bronchodilator hasn't provided sufficient treatment.

Symptoms of asthma include shortness of breath, tightness in the chest, a wheezing sound which develops when breathing and coughing that may worsen due to a possible virus.

The most severe cases of asthma, particularly those involving status asthmaticus, can result in cyanosis, tachypnea, syncope, hypertension or seizures.

Asthma may be triggered by exercise, occupational activities or allergies.

Asthma may be diagnosed through a chest X-ray. Additionally, the scan can confirm whether a patient is suffering from pneumonia. Pulse oximetry may identify the carbon dioxide saturation in the patient's blood.

Blood sugar testing may also be used as a form of diagnosis, given that patients with asthma may develop hyperglycemia. Younger patients may also experience hypoglycemia.

Possible treatments for asthma include:

- Beta2-agonists – relax the muscles in the airways. This allows the bronchial airways to expand, thus permitting air to flow to the lungs.
- Anticholinergics – block the production of acetylcholine, which leads to the dilation of the bronchial airways and eases breathing.
- Corticosteroids – resolve inflammation caused by asthma, although they should only be used for brief periods of time.
- Methylxanthines – may restore bronchial functions, although drug blood levels must be carefully monitored to confirm the asthmatic concerns are being properly controlled.
- Magnesium sulfate – relaxes muscles in the lungs, thus improving the bronchodilation process.
- Heliox (a mixture of helium and oxygen) – may be administered through a face mask to relieve the airways. This makes it easier for the patient to breathe.

It is possible for some patients' asthma to be fully resolved. However, asthma can remain dormant for years at a time and then return, triggered by a variety of conditions as described above.

Epiglottitis

Epiglottitis is the inflammation of the epiglottis. The epiglottis is the piece of cartilage that moves over the windpipe when a person swallows, to prevent the aspiration of food.

Epiglottitis is generally caused by a bacterial infection such as streptococcus pneumonia.

A patient may develop a fever, sore throat, change in voice, cyanosis, tachypnea and/or hypoxia.

A laryngoscope is the primary tool used for identifying the condition. The epiglottis will be bright red when infected, a condition that is readily visible when using the scope.

Epiglottis may be fatal if not swiftly treated. Intravenously administered antibiotics may be used as treatment, along with NSAIDs such as ibuprofen.

A tracheostomy may be necessary in cases where a patient's airway needs to be swiftly opened to allow breathing. Beta2-agonists may also be used, although the effectiveness of the treatment will vary based on the situation.

Tracheitis

Tracheitis is an inflammation in the trachea. The condition develops mainly in children, although some adults may also be at risk.

Tracheitis may be triggered by an upper respiratory infection. Symptoms may include a rough cough, a fever, wheezing and a general hoarse feeling in the throat.

A pulse oximetry test may be used to assess a patient's lung function. Sometimes an X-ray of the neck may also be used for diagnostic purposes.

This condition may be fatal if not swiftly treated. Intravenously administered antibiotics are critical for treatment. A tracheostomy is not required unless the airways cannot be opened any other way. Fever reducers may also be prescribed.

Inhalation Injury

An inhalation injury occurs when a person inhales any of various outside materials that might irritate the epithelium such as sulfur dioxide, chlorine, ozone and hydrogen chloride. This may have a negative impact on the airway, causing a person to struggle with breathing.

There may be no exterior signs of an inhalation injury. A patient may experience rhinitis, wheezing and frequent productive coughs. The mouth may develop a burning sensation. Nasal hairs may also appear to be damaged, and could even look singed.

A chest X-ray is recommended as the primary diagnostic tool. A CT scan, pulse oximetry and pulmonary function test may also be indicated, depending on the severity of the condition.

Supplemental oxygen may be used as part of the standard treatment process, but the oxygen must be fully humidified. IV fluids are also helpful, particularly for patients who have burns as a result of the foreign substance they inhaled. Albuterol may help ease a patient's breathing.

Hyperbaric oxygen therapy is best for those who have experienced carbon monoxide poisoning.

Airway Obstruction

An airway obstruction occurs when the respiratory tract becoming blocked. Some air may still be able to pass through in some cases, but there may also be times when the airways are completely obstructed so a patient can no longer breathe.

An obstruction may be the result of an allergic reaction (anaphylaxis) when the airway swells shut due to a reaction to certain antibiotics or allergens such as peanuts.

A patient who experiences an obstruction will display cyanosis, tachycardia, swelling in the face and tongue and may be confused. Additionally, there may be no breathing sounds if the patient's airway is fully obstructed. If a person is choking, he or she may soon become unconscious if treatment is not swiftly administered.

The Heimlich maneuver is necessary for patients who are choking on foreign objects.

For other cases, a CT scan or X-ray should be performed on the patient's chest and neck in order to determine what is causing the obstruction and where, exactly, it is located.

A tracheostomy is necessary for a complete obstruction, along with supplemental oxygen.

For cases of anaphylaxis, anti-inflammatory medication should be provided. Antihistamines and other such medications may be useful.

Pleural Effusion

A pleural effusion occurs when more than 10 ml of pleural fluid builds up in the pleural space, between the parietal and visceral pleurae in the lungs.

In this situation, the ratio of fluid to serum protein will be greater than 0.5, while the ratio of fluid to serum LDH will be more than 0.6. A thoracentesis may be used to aspirate fluid from the chest. This can help relieve a patient's breathing. Additionally, the fluid's cell count, pH total and differentials should be measured.

A tube thoracostomy, also known as a chest tube solution, is necessary in cases where breathing is difficult. Pleurodesis produces an irritant that causes inflammation to clear out the pleural space, thus potentially removing the excess fluid. Proper monitoring is needed after the treatment process in order to ensure that the pleural fluid that has been removed does not build up again.

Pneumothorax

A pneumothorax occurs when there is no air in the pleural cavity. The condition may take one of three forms:

1. Spontaneous

A spontaneous pneumothorax occurs when a patient does not have a history of this condition. Prior lung disease can increase a patient's likelihood of developing the issue. A person who has lung cancer may be at a higher risk for the condition.

2. Traumatic

A person who experiences a significant physical injury to the chest, such as penetration by an object, has a risk of developing a traumatic pneumothorax. A surgical procedure is often necessary, depending upon the severity of the injury. Blunt-force trauma is also a cause.

3. Tension

A tension pneumothorax occurs when, due to some form of trauma upon the chest wall, air is trapped in the pleural space under a positive amount of pressure. This pressure upon the lungs can make it very hard for a person to breathe.

Symptoms of a tension pneumothorax include chest pains, cyanosis, tachycardia, hypotension or difficulty breathing. Because of the level of discomfort a tension pneumothorax can cause, patients may also suffer from anxiety.

A chest CT scan, ultrasonography or X-ray may be used to diagnose the condition.

In most cases, supplemental oxygen is enough to treat the tension pneumothorax. A patient's condition will need to be monitored as he or she recovers.

In some cases, depending on the severity of the patient's condition, a chest tube, thoracostomy or simple needle aspiration may be required. If these treatments are required, they should be performed swiftly.

Pulmonary Edema

Pulmonary edema, also known as "wet lung," occurs when there is an excess of fluid built up in the air sacs within the lungs, therefore making it hard for a patient to breathe. Heart disease may trigger pulmonary edema, along with trauma or certain medications. People who take aspirin regularly may be at a higher risk for the condition.

Acute pulmonary edema will display short-term effects such as gasping, shortness of breath, a cold sensation or anxiety. A chronic long-term issue has symptoms which include difficulty breathing when exerting one's self or when lying flat, and sudden weight gain.

People in high-altitude conditions are more prone to pulmonary edema. Headaches are often the first signs of edema. Coughing, difficulty walking uphill, fatigue and fever can develop.

A blood test, pulse oximetry or electrocardiogram may be used to help diagnose pulmonary edema. A pulmonary artery catheterization process may also be used to assess lung function. A wedge pressure under 18 mm Hg may be interpreted as a sign of edema, particularly noncancerous edema.

When a patient presents with pulmonary edema, supplementary oxygen should be swiftly administered. In severe cases, a hyperbaric chamber may be required.

If a patient is anxious, morphine may be advisable, but a physician should always be consulted first as morphine may interfere with breathing, thereby worsening the problem.

Pulmonary Embolism

A pulmonary embolism (PE) is a blood clot (also known as a thrombus) that occurs in the lungs. A PE may develop due to a deep vein thrombosis (DVT) clot breaking apart and entering the lungs. Sometimes the clot may occur in the pelvis, kidneys or other parts of the body.

A PE can be deadly if not swiftly treated. If treatment isn't rapidly administered, it may cause lung failure. Virchow's triad states that thrombosis develops due to:

1. How well blood coagulates; excess coagulation is a threat
2. Endothelial functionality; any cases where the system is not working well are a danger to a person's health
3. Blood stasis

A patient who is immobile for long periods of time may develop DVT, possibly followed by a PE. Surgery and obesity can raise the risk of a blood clot developing.

A PE can trigger breathing difficulties and a persistent cough. Cyanosis or hypoxia may also occur.

A patient's pulmonary system should be assessed when he or she presents with a possible PE. Cyanosis, tachypnea, fever and edema may be present. A cardiac murmur may also occur in some cases. A CT scan can help with assessing lung functionality.

A D-dimer blood test can help diagnose a PE. The test involves assessing the protein fragments present in the blood after a clot breaks apart. A test with a high D-dimer total suggests that the patient has a high risk of a PE, or may be experiencing an episode.

A PE requires immediate treatment as the condition is fatal if untreated. Supplemental oxygen should be administered swiftly. Dopamine or dobutamine should be intravenously administered in order to help regulate a patient's blood pressure. A patient will require proper ventilation, sometimes with full mechanical support in order to prevent further damage. Throughout the treatment, cardiac monitoring must be in place.

Thrombolytics may be administered to destroy the clot. Hypotensive patients in particular will require this medication. Anticoagulants may also be administered to prevent clots from developing and to remove any existing clots that might persist. Bleeding may develop in the treatment process due to the medication dissolving the blood clots.

Surgery is not necessary unless other treatments are not helping. An embolectomy is a surgical procedure to remove the PE. A catheter may be surgically inserted into the blood vessel and used to break apart a clot if necessary. Since this is a surgical procedure, it should only be performed if other treatments aren't helping or the clot is becoming a danger to the patient's well-being.

Blood thinners may be prescribed to control PE. Such medications are particularly useful after a surgical procedure or when DVT is being simultaneously treated in a person. Thrombolytics may also be prescribed, but only in severe cases as they may cause sudden bleeding to develop in some cases.

Respiratory Distress Syndrome

Respiratory distress syndrome (RDS) occurs when the alveoli capillaries develop inflammation, leading to rapid pulmonary failure. The condition may occur at random and can impact both adults and children.

The intensity of respiratory distress syndrome may be measured using the PaO_2/FiO_2 ratio based on five centimeters of continuous positive airway pressure (CPAP). The PaO_2 total is the partial pressure of oxygen. FiO_2 is the fraction of inspired oxygen.

RDS is mild when the PaO2/FiO2 ratio is from 200 to 300. The condition is moderate when the ratio is from 100 to 200. The issue is severe if the ratio is under or equal to 100.

RDS may be triggered by sepsis, pneumonia, inhalation of fumes or trauma. A person who has undergone a significant blood transfusion may also be at elevated risk of developing the condition. There is a potential for patients with RDS not to display any kind of immediately visible symptoms anywhere from 24 to 48 hours after the event that caused the problem.

Dyspnea may develop upon exertion, although the issue will eventually develop even when the patient is at rest. Hypotension can occur alongside intense fatigue. The patient's heart rate will eventually drop.

RDS is a potentially fatal condition and requires rapid intervention. The mortality rate is greater among older individuals. Whether young or old, patients may require hospitalization depending upon the severity of the case.

A clinical exam is necessary in order to confirm RDS. This includes a chest X-ray to identify any lung infiltrates, and an ABG analysis to diagnose cases of extreme hypoxemia. A bronchoscopy may be performed to confirm that the condition is not being caused by a lung infection.

Corticosteroids, simvastatin and ibuprofen may be administered in order to ease the discomfort of a patient's symptoms. Intubation and medical ventilation should be used. A broad-spectrum antibiotic may also be administered to lessen the risk of sepsis developing during the treatment process.

A patient may require hydration to replace lost fluids. This should only be done after ventilation, when a patient is clearly responding to treatment.

Injuries to the Pulmonary System

Any injury to the pulmonary system should be assessed as either blunt-force trauma or penetrative. Treatment will vary based upon the type of injury and its severity.

Contusion

A contusion is a deep bruise within the lung tissue, resulting due to chest trauma. The alveoli will swell and collect blood, impacting lung function.

The symptoms of a lung contusion will develop 24 to 48 hours after the initial chest injury. The lungs will collect blood in the process, causing symptoms including dyspnea, hypoxia, chest pains, hypotension and tachycardia. A general loss of blood may also develop.

A chest X-ray can be used to identify a contusion. Pulse oximetry may be used to assess lung functionality in order to determine the extent of the injury.

Supplemental oxygen may be provided to treat hypoxia. Analgesics may be useful to treat any pain resulting from the injury.

A patient's fluids should be monitored. Mechanical ventilation is only necessary in the most severe cases, such as when the patient is not responding to other treatments.

Hemothorax

A hemothorax develops due to a penetrating injury. Blood enters the pleural space, impairing lung function. As a result, chest pains and tachypnea are likely to occur. A patient's blood pressure may also drop.

A chest X-ray is useful in pinpointing the location of the injury. It can also assess which part of the lung has been most impacted.

The severity of a hemothorax will vary based on the injury and some cases may resolve without intervention. In other situations, a tube thoracotomy may be required. A needle aspiration is not indicated for a hemothorax as it will not remove enough blood to relieve the patient.

A bacterial infection may develop during the treatment process due to a blood clot. Broad-spectrum antibiotics may be prescribed to prevent such an infection from occurring.

Flail Chest

Flail chest develops when the chest wall is damaged and ribs are fractured. Such fractures may limit the overall flexibility of the lungs, thus preventing the patient from being able to breathe properly.

As a result of injury—typically blunt force—ribs will float up from the chest wall, impeding lung function.

Patients who have been in car accidents or who have been physically assaulted are at greater risk of developing flail chest.

A visual assessment of the chest should be enough to diagnose flail chest. A CT scan or chest X-ray may also help with monitoring the situation or can be used to confirm the condition. A breathing test may also be performed to assess a patient's lung function.

Supplemental oxygen can be provided to the patient at the start of the treatment process. The broken bones must be treated appropriately. Mechanical ventilation may be of assistance. A thoracotomy may be necessary in cases where the lungs are fatigued as a result of flail chest.

Antibiotics may be prescribed to prevent the risk of pneumonia. To further prevent infection, a patient should be kept in a sterile environment while in recovery.

Rib Fracture

A rib fracture involves an injury to the rib cage that occurs after blunt-force trauma. One or more ribs may be fractured. Causes of rib fractures include car accidents and sports injuries.

It's vital to note the number of the fractured ribs as this relates to the ribs' position in the chest and can indicate what kind of pulmonary trauma may result. A rib fracture may entail one of the following:

1. A vessel, the trachea or bronchus could be injured if the first or second rib is fractured
2. The fourth to seventh ribs, while they may cause significant pain if fractured, should not impact lung function or other parts of the body
3. The eighth rib or lower may cause additional pain. If the right side is injured, the liver may be damaged. If the injury is on the left side, the spleen may be damaged.

Changes in the chest wall, tenderness in the area and difficulty breathing may result from a rib fracture.

A chest X-ray should be used to diagnose the rib fracture. A patient's pulmonary system should also be assessed.

A patient may receive supplemental oxygen and incentive spirometry as a part of his or her treatment. NSAIDs may help with pain and inflammation.

The risk of lung complications due to a rib fracture is lower in younger patients. People over the age of 65 have a greater risk of complications after suffering a rib fracture.

Tracheal Injury

A tracheal injury may cause intense pain. The trauma in the area may be triggered by an infection, although general trauma may be a concern for some patients. The patient may experience emphysema-like symptoms.

A chest X-ray may be used to assess the severity of the injury. A CT scan can also be used to determine how deep the injury is.

Mechanical ventilation is often necessary to maintain a patient's airway function. A thoracostomy process may be required to help drain any excess fluids that may pool in the region, including blood.

A bronchoscopy is necessary if there are any solid items in the area such as a bullet. Antibiotics can be prescribed to prevent a possible infection from developing in the trachea.

Diaphragm Injury

A diaphragm injury results in harm to the thoracic cavity, possibly due to a penetrating injury.

A patient with a diaphragm injury will experience significant difficulties in breathing. A chest X-ray can help in identifying the severity of the damage.

Surgery is necessary to treat an injured diaphragm, in order to give a patient the best chances for a trouble-free recovery. Antibiotics may also be prescribed to prevent infection.

Chapter 5 – Cardiovascular and Hematological Health

The cardiovascular system includes the heart and involves the circulation of blood throughout the human body. The following chapter focuses on understanding the anatomical considerations for the cardiovascular system and the various conditions that may impair its function.

Anatomical Analysis

Circulation

The circulation process is critical to cardiovascular health. Circulation moves blood through the body in the following manner:

1. Arteries move oxygenated blood from the heart towards the rest of the body.
2. The aorta takes in blood from the left ventricle of the heart. Oxygen-rich blood moves through the rest of the body.
3. The blood ends at the arterioles that go into the capillary bed.
4. The capillary beds drain through the venules.
5. The non-oxygenated blood circulates back to the right atrium. Various larger veins help return the blood.
6. The blood is then pumped to the lungs via the pulmonary artery, oxygenating the blood.
7. The oxygenated blood moves from the pulmonary vein to the left atrium and then to the aorta. The full cycle repeats.

Proper circulation is vital to preventing changes of blood pressure in the body. Heart failure is likely to occur in cases where circulation is impaired. The supply of oxygenated blood to the body's tissues is critical to a human's well-being and any impairment must be swiftly treated.

Arteries

The arteries are critical to moving blood throughout the body.

An artery has a thick middle layer that helps to prevent blood pressure changes. The tunica media in the middle includes smooth muscle fibers. Connective tissues, called the tunica externa, make up the flexible exterior of the artery, keeping it supple.

The types of arteries are:

1. Elastic

An elastic artery takes blood directly from the heart. The aorta and pulmonary arteries are examples of elastic arteries.

2. Muscular

A muscular artery distributes blood to various parts of the body. The coronary and femoral arteries are both examples of muscular arteries. Such arteries feature more smooth muscle to help them relax or contract when blood moves through.

3. Arterioles

Arterioles are small branches of arteries that move blood to the capillaries. The tunica media includes smooth muscle necessary to contract or dilate the flow of blood.

Veins

Veins are blood vessels that move blood to the heart. Types of veins include:

1. Pulmonary

Pulmonary veins move oxygenated blood from the lungs toward the left atrium.

2. Systemic

Systemic veins move non-oxygenated blood to the right atrium.

3. Superficial

Superficial veins are near the skin's surface and are not near any other arteries. Such veins may include added blood, although the proper functionality of the vein should be identified accordingly.

4. Deep

Deep veins are inside the muscle tissue, located near other arteries. The name of a particular vein links up to the artery; this can include a coronary vein. Such veins may be difficult to treat in cases of malfunction.

These veins feature the same layers that are found in other blood-carrying surfaces inside the body. The tunica adventitia is the outside covering, while the tunica media is the middle layer. The tunica intima, the inside part, has elastic tissues to facilitate blood flow.

All veins work together to ensure the circulatory system is functioning smoothly.

Aorta

The aorta runs from the left ventricle in the heart through the diaphragm and into the pelvis and abdomen. It moves into two separate arteries that circulate blood to the legs and lower trunk.

Brain Circulation and the Circle of Willis

The internal carotid artery is responsible for delivering blood to the brain. The artery moves into the cranium and then divides up into a series of arteries called the Circle of Willis.

The Circle of Willis comprises the following features:

1. The anterior cerebral artery links to the anterior communicating artery at the top.
2. The middle cerebral artery corresponds with the anterior choroidal artery.
3. A series of posterior arteries allow blood to move through the heart.
4. A basilar artery appears at the end to facilitate the flow of blood.

Spleen

While often viewed as unnecessary since it may be removed if needed, the spleen is nevertheless a vital part of the cardiovascular system. The spleen filters red blood cells, removing old cells.

The spleen also produces white blood cells responsible for controlling infections. The white blood cells also facilitate the development of antibodies.

Heart Layers

The heart is made of several layers. Individual segments may affect heart function in different ways. These include cases where certain parts might develop inflammation or other concerns, thus potentially harming the functionality of the entire heart muscle:

1. Pericardium

The pericardium is the outside layer of the heart. It forms the sac that protects the heart.

2. Myocardium

The myocardium is the middle, largest layer of the heart. The myocardium requires oxygen for proper functionality. A myocardial infarction occurs when not enough oxygen reaches the heart.

3. Endocardium

The endocardium is the inside part of the heart. The layer comprises the heart's chambers and its valves. Endocarditis develops when the layer becomes inflamed. An infection may be triggered by the staphylococci or streptococci bacteria.

The Electrical Functionality of the Heart Muscle

The heart muscle must be capable of producing the proper beats in order to maintain the correct circulatory function. The electrical functionality is vital to the heart's health.

The Conduction Process

The conduction process is the process by which the heart beats. The process entails the following steps:

1. An electric impulse goes from the sinoatrial node to the aorta walls. As a result, the walls contract.
2. The impulse reaches the atrioventricular node. The impulse occurs after a brief delay.
3. Bundle branches move signals from the atrioventricular node to the peak area of the heart.
4. The signal moves through the ventricle walls. The walls contract, thus producing a heartbeat.

An electrocardiogram (ECG) can be used to assess a heart's electrical function.

Noting the Electrical Wave In the Heart's Operational Process

A heart's electrical wave should be measured as follows:

1. P wave
2. Atrial contraction; a small hump appears between this and the P wave
3. Q wave; the electrical readout goes down slightly
4. R wave; this should be the highest point on the cycle readout

5. S wave; this should be around the same depth as the Q wave
6. ST segment; the ventricles contract to create a stable line
7. Repolarization, which occurs when the T wave produces a slight hump
8. At this point, the beat returns to its original value

The waves should be consistent and regular throughout the ECG readout. Any unusual changes may threaten the health of the heart and should be swiftly addressed.

How Cardiac Cells Function

There are four aspects of how cardiac cells function:

1. Excitability

The heart responds to external stimuli and operates as it should.

2. Conductivity

An electrical impulse should be easy to transport. The action must start at the SA node and move along cardiac cells.

3. Contractility

The cardiac cells should be able to move an action potential to the mechanical efforts for contraction and relaxation.

4. Automaticity

Cardiac cells can move without having to be stimulated by the nerves. The heart can trigger an impulse on its own. This effort is known as automaticity. The AV node may produce the impulse if the SA cannot do so, though the AV node's impulse will be slower. Other cells in the heart will start an action if the AV node fails, but those cells will also be slower.

All four of these functions work on the action potential generated within the heart. The potential refers to the changes in voltage in a cardiac cell. Ions move through the potassium, calcium and sodium channels. The ions trigger cardiac muscle fiber contractions, which occur following electrical activity.

The flow from the sodium (Na+) channel moves through, thus increasing the membrane potential. Calcium (Ca+) moves through, while potassium (K+) clears out. After this, the membrane potential starts to drop. It takes less than half a second on average for the action to occur. The P and T waves on the ECG readout reveal how the effort takes place.

Any changes in how well the process works may be a sign of a heartbeat-related issue. A person might experience significant changes in how the heart functions as a result. There is a potential for the heart to stop working if such problems are not resolved as soon as possible.

Conditions of Note

Cardiovascular and hematological health issues relate to the myocardium, the heart muscle.

In most emergency situations, an ECG should be performed to identify how well a patient's heart is functioning. Additional tests that may be needed will be discussed in this chapter. Intravenous lines may be required for some patients to provide appropriate replacement of fluids of various sorts.

Endocarditis

Endocarditis is a condition where the heart valve experiences inflammation. As a result, bacteria and other compounds from another part of the body may then enter the heart valve.

Bacteria are likely to develop in the area due to another medical procedure. A patient who undergoes a colonoscopy or a regular dental cleaning might be at a higher risk of contracting endocarditis. During the treatment, bacteria may enter the bloodstream and eventually reach the heart.

A patient may develop chills, fever, fatigue and/or a heart murmur.

The condition may spread fast, depending on the type of bacteria. Staphylococcus bacteria will cause endocarditis to develop faster.

Antibiotic treatment should help if the condition becomes severe. Valve replacement surgery may be required if the condition is not responding, or the damage is significant.

It can take around four to six weeks for the condition to resolve with treatment. Failure to control the condition may result in damage to the heart and a possible stroke.

Pericarditis

Pericarditis occurs as a result of trauma to the chest or heart muscle. As a result, the pericardium develops inflammation and the fluid between the layers of the pericardium is impacted, allowing additional friction to develop between the two parts. Lupus, rheumatoid arthritis or other inflammatory disorders may also contribute to the condition.

Pericarditis may produce sharp pains and heart palpitations. A patient may cough intensely or develop a low-grade fever.

Pericarditis may be diagnosed by using an ECG, a chest X-ray or CT scan.

Pain relief medications such as aspirin or ibuprofen can be prescribed to the patient. Colchicine may also be prescribed to reduce the intensity of the inflammation. Corticosteroids such as prednisone may also help manage symptoms.

A pericardiectomy is only necessary if the pericardium's function is not restored via other forms of treatment.

Myocarditis

Myocarditis occurs when the myocardium becomes inflamed. The heart's electrical system is negatively influenced, impacting its regular rhythm.

Myocarditis is caused by viral infections in most cases. The condition may also be triggered by a drug reaction. Some parasites can also cause the issue, although such cases are more likely to be seen in South America.

Myocarditis causes a fever, fainting and breathing difficulties. Arrhythmias may also develop in some situations. Failure to treat myocarditis can result in a heart attack.

An ECG will identify changes in heart rhythms. A chest X-ray and MRI may also help diagnose the condition.

ACE inhibitors or beta-blockers may help with treating pain. Intravenous medications may also be administered to treat the condition.

An intra-aortic balloon pump may be inserted into the heart. A catheter is threaded into a blood vessel in the leg and then guided to the heart. A balloon at the end of the catheter is inflated as needed. As a result, blood flow to the heart is restored and its function will improve.

Types of Myocardial Infarctions

A myocardial infarction affects the heart's overall functionality. Some conditions may be asymptomatic, and eventually can lead to significant health crises without much warning.

Acute Coronary Syndrome

Acute coronary syndrome (ACS), also known as acute myocardial ischemia, involves a lack of blood flow to the heart.

An ECG may show an uneven layout in between heartbeats. While the intervals or segments between heartbeats should be consistent, there may be cases where there is an elevation of energy or power in between beats.

Chest pains will be prominent, and may extend well beyond the heart area and into the arms, neck and back. A patient may also experience changes in consciousness, nausea, palpitations or feel a shortness of breath.

Blood thinners or beta-blockers may be prescribed. Coronary artery bypass surgery may be required in the most severe cases, especially if medications are not working as well as hoped.

Cardiopulmonary Arrest

Cardiopulmonary arrest occurs when the heart muscle stops functioning. The condition is triggered by a significant change in the electrical functions within the heart.

The cardiopulmonary arrest event often occurs as electric signals are disrupted. The regular functionality of the heart entails an electric impulse moving from the sinoatrial node to the atria walls. During a cardiopulmonary arrest, the heart does not receive the impulse correctly.

Defibrillation is necessary to restore the heart's normal function. The sooner defibrillation can be administered, the better chance a patient has of surviving cardiopulmonary arrest.

Dysrhythmia

Dysrhythmia is a change in the electrical activity in the heart. The sudden change may be due to the heart beating too fast, slow or irregularly. The change occurs when there is a disruption in the regular conduction cycle within the heart.

A calcium channel blocker or beta-blocker may be prescribed. A pacemaker or other implantable device that defibrillates the heart may also be necessary.

Sinus Bradycardia

Sinus bradycardia develops when the SA node produces a beat rate at under 60 beats per minute. Metabolic distress may be responsible for the condition.

Patients who take calcium channel blockers or beta-blocker medications are at an elevated risk of developing the condition.

Atropine may be prescribed to resolve the situation. Transcutaneous pacing may also be utilized to stabilize the heart's function.

Sinus Tachycardia

Sinus tachycardia is when the SA node produces an unusually fast heart rate. The rate may be 100 beats per minute or greater.

Shock or heart failure may trigger sinus tachycardia. Illegal drug use may also be a factor. The condition is particularly noticeable among those who use cocaine. It's important to determine the reason for the condition, as that may affect treatment.

Ivabradine may be administered as a form of treatment. The patient should be warned not to consume or use any possible triggers such as alcohol or nicotine. Beta-blockers or calcium channel blockers may also help treat the condition, but they should be monitored to ensure they do not produce more of an effect than desired.

Supraventricular Tachycardia

SVT occurs when an AV nodal reentry circuit develops and a person's heart rate reaches anywhere from 150 to 250 beats per minute.

A carotid massage may help to lower the heart rate. Beta-blockers can also be prescribed, but the patient must be monitored to ensure the medication is producing the desired effect.

Atrial Fibrillation

Atrial fibrillation (Afib) occurs when many foci in the atria function at the same time. This causes the heart to beat irregularly. The sudden change may not be very fast, and it's difficult to identify without an appropriate ECG exam.

A patient may experience fatigue, chest pains or hypotension. Most of these symptoms may not be easily noticeable until a significant cardiac episode occurs, thus making regular exams critical.

An ECG may reveal Afib based on how each wave changes in intensity. A person with Afib may have some waves that are much higher than others or which are+ visibly irregular.

Beta-blockers and cardioversion may be used as forms of treatment.

Atrial Flutter

An atrial flutter occurs when an atrial focus fires from 250 to 350 times per minute. The flutter can be seen in an ECG through the many peaks and valleys occurring on a readout at shorter intervals.

Cardioversion treatment is recommended. The treatment entails administering electric shocks to the chest in order to restore the heart's natural function.

Ventricular Tachycardia

Ventricular tachycardia (V-tach) develops when a single ventricular focus produces signals. The rate can go from 150 to 250 beats per minute. As a result, the heart may experience stress. An ECG readout will show the peaks in the heart becoming irregular, without much rest involved.

Lidocaine or procainamide should be administered. An implantable cardioverter defibrillator may also be required.

Ventricular Fibrillation

Ventricular fibrillation (Vfib) entails many ventricular ectopic foci contracting at the same time.

An ECG readout will show radically irregular heartbeats. There will be no clear pattern to the patient's heartbeat.

Defibrillation is required to resolve Vfib. Lidocaine may also be administered during the treatment process.

Torsades de Pointes

Torsades de pointes occurs when the QT interview on an ECG readout is prolonged. The heart may be severely impacted. Magnesium is recommended for treatment.

Heart Blocks

A heart block, also known as bradycardia, develops when the heart is not beating fast enough. The episode can entail a first-, second- or third-degree block.

A first-degree block occurs when the SA node impulse is slow. The P and R waves will be longer. The first-degree block is the mildest issue that may develop, although it might result in more significant problems.

A second-degree block involves the impulses on the SA node being delayed or the beat being skipped altogether. The PR interval will become increasingly longer to where the P wave is no longer being supported well.

A third-degree block is a complete block. In such a situation, the SA node operates from 80 to 100 beats per minute, but the impulses are not reaching the ventricles. The beats produced will be less than half of the norm. A temporary pacemaker may be required to resolve the block.

Angina

Angina is chest pain produced by a lack of blood flow to the heart muscle.

Angina can be stable or unstable. Stable angina involves predictable, consistent chest pain. The patient may be at risk of a heart attack in the future, but it may also be a less strenuous condition to contend with.

Unstable angina entails random pain, often without any physical activity involved. Unstable angina may abruptly become more severe. The condition should be treated as an emergency, as it suggests that a heart attack is likely to develop at any moment.

A patient may report feeling heaviness or tightness in his or chest. The pain may become intense.

A patient with angina should be encouraged to make proper dietary changes. Appropriate exercise may also be encouraged, although a personal trainer might need to be consulted to figure out the safest exercise routine.

Medications may also help with the treatment of the condition. Such medications can include beta-blockers or calcium channel blockers. Such medications may help with reducing the patient's blood pressure, thus lessening the risk for angina to develop.

A cholesterol test may also be indicated to assess how the treatment is progressing. High LDL or low HDL cholesterol totals may be a sign of possible angina.

For stable angina, nitroglycerin helps to control the condition. The medication dilates blood vessels, thus facilitating blood flow.

For unstable angina, surgical treatment may be necessary. A coronary artery bypass grafting surgery may be necessary. A cholesterol control medication or antiplatelet medication may be required.

NSTEMI

A non-ST-elevation myocardial infarction is a heart attack that is identified by the ST segment in an electrocardiogram. The ST segment will not experience any significant changes. The issue may cause significant damage to the heart muscle if not correctly treated.

ACE inhibitors, beta-blockers or antiplatelet medications may be recommended for treatment.

STEMI

An ST-elevation myocardial infarction entails a dramatic shift in the ST segment on the ECG readout. The coronary artery will experience a complete blockage, preventing blood flow. This can cause significant damage to the affected body part if not swiftly treated.

Aneurysm-Related Concerns

An aneurysm may develop in many heart-related situations.

Aneurysm

An aneurysm is a swelling that occurs in an artery. The aneurysm can occur in various parts of the body, although the left ventricle is the most common site. An aorta may also develop an aneurysm. In rare cases, aneurysms may develop in the brain.

An aneurysm will be visible as a bulge or ballooning effect occurring on the side of an artery. The bulge will eventually rupture, thus causing leaking throughout the artery.

A patient with an aneurysm may experience pain in the chest and surrounding areas. A headache may also develop in some cases. The symptoms will not be noticeable until the aneurysm ruptures.

Stenting and embolization are necessary in the area where the aneurysm is found in order to prevent further bleeding. A vascular grafting procedure may be required to seal the rupture. Blood thinners may be required after the procedure, in order to ease stress on a patient's arteries.

Left Ventricular Aneurysm

A heart attack may trigger a left ventricular aneurysm (LVA.) The condition does not produce any symptoms and must be diagnosed through an angiogram. Although some LVAs may not require treatment, others might develop clots and could require intervention. In such cases, anticoagulant medications may be prescribed.

Aneurysm Dissection

A dissection is a part of the aneurysm where the arterial wall layers become separated. As a result, blood will start to leak between multiple layers of the artery.

The affected artery will remain functional, but the leakage will weaken how efficient the artery is in helping to circulate blood through the body.

Beta-blockers may be prescribed to help neutralize the leakage.

Ruptured Aorta

In severe cases, a rupture, also known as a thoracic aortic aneurysm, may develop in the aorta. This occurs when there is a weakening in the upper part of the aorta.

The rupture will trigger tenderness in the chest. Back pains may also develop. Some people may feel a shortness of breath due to the added stress imposed on the heart. The condition may produce sharp pains that can radiate throughout the body and which could potentially cause further discomfort if not treated accordingly.

A chest X-ray can help diagnose the condition. An ECG may also assist in identifying the specific part of the heart where the issue has developed.

There is a potential for the rupture to heal on its own, but treatment is nevertheless recommended. Beta-blockers or statins may be prescribed.

In other cases, a surgical procedure could be required. Open-heart surgery to implant a graft on the artery may be necessary. A catheter may also be inserted through an endovascular process. The type of surgery will vary depending on the severity of the condition.

Heart Failure

Heart failure occurs when the heart muscle is unable to support the metabolic functions necessary for regular operation. This condition may be fatal if left untreated. The situation may develop both suddenly and gradually. Long-term issues may trigger weaknesses in the heart that eventually lead to overall failure.

Forms of Heart Failure

Heart failure can occur in many forms. It is important to determine where the failure occurred, as this affects treatment.

1. Left-sided

Left-sided heart failure occurs when the left ventricle is unable to produce enough oxygen-rich blood. The failure of the left ventricle causes blood to back up in the lungs, thus producing a buildup of fluids and shortness of breath.

2. Right-sided

Right-sided heart failure occurs when the right ventricle cannot function correctly. Damage to the left ventricle may trigger the failure. As the lungs fill with blood, this makes it harder for the right ventricle to function as the ventricle requires extra pressure for operation.

A person's lower extremities will develop intense swelling in the legs and feet as a result of the fluid backup.

3. Diastolic

Diastolic heart failure occurs as the heart muscle becomes stiffer than usual and is unable to fill with blood as well as it should. The blood will become unable to flow to other parts of the body due to the condition. This form of heart failure is more likely to occur among women.

4. Systolic

Systolic heart failure occurs when the heart muscle is no longer capable of contracting. The condition occurs when the heart is enlarged. Systolic heart failure occurs mainly among men.

General Signs and Risks

Patients who experience anemia, emphysema or thyroid production issues are at a higher risk of developing heart failure. People who are overweight, smoke or have unhealthy diets may also be at high risk.

In some cases, a patient may not notice heart failure until a heart attack occurs. The issue may entail intense chest pain and discomfort, a cold or numb feeling in the upper part of the body, intense fatigue and dizziness or nausea. A rapid heart rate may also occur due to the condition.

A patient may also experience pulmonary congestion. In this case, a cough will develop and the patient will have a hard time breathing while lying down. The patient may also start to feel tired and anxious throughout the day, with the condition worsening at night.

Most symptoms are gradual and occur over time. Others may suddenly develop, depending on the heart's overall health.

Testing Process

An ECG may identify issues within the heart. A chest X-ray can also help identify specific parts of the heart that might be malfunctioning.

A stress exam can be administered if the patient is capable of handling such exertion. The exam requires the patient to perform an exercise, usually on a treadmill. The patient is monitored to see how well his or her body responds to stress.

General Measurements

Heart failure can be measured through a patient's cardiac output. The cardiac output is the heart rate multiplied by the stroke volume, the total amount of blood produced out of the ventricles for every beat.

The systemic vascular resistance (SVR) is a measure of the ability of blood to move through the vessels. The SVR will increase when the vessels appear narrow and stiff, or the blood that moves through becomes too thick. The aortic valve will thus struggle to function.

The pulmonary vascular resistance (PVR) is another measurement to note. The PVR is the difference between the pulmonary arterial pressure and the left atrial filling pressure. The resistance that the heart experiences may influence how well the PVR may be measured.

A preload can also be used to take the measure of the ventricular stretch around the end part of the diastole where the chambers fill. The preload is a measure of the pressure of blood against the left ventricle. The afterload entails the resistance that the heart has to overcome to allow the aortic valve to open, thus allowing blood to move into the systemic circulation. The goal for the treatment of heart failure should be to reduce the afterload involved.

Treatment Options

A coronary bypass or angioplasty may be required depending on the severity of the condition and on whether there is any arterial blockage. An implantable pacemaker may be necessary for patients whose hearts' electrical function is not working properly.

Vasodilators or ACE inhibitors may also help improve a heart's function. Patients who are prescribed these medications will require monitoring to ensure the condition is responding appropriately.

A heart transplant is only necessary if other treatments have failed to function and a patient has suffered severe, permanent damage to his or her heart. There is no guarantee that a heart transplant will actually work, so it is a last resort.

Patients should be encouraged to exercise, eat healthily, moderate alcohol consumption and avoid smoking.

Blood Pressure Concerns

Blood pressure is measured as the amount of blood the heart pumps and the resistance of the blood flow in the arteries. The blood pressure total increases when the heart pumps more blood and the arteries narrow. Both high and low blood pressure can cause health problems.

Hypertension

Hypertension is a condition where blood imposes excess force along the artery walls. The condition may weaken the walls, thus leading to heart failure, among other concerns.

Hypertension (high blood pressure) is diagnosed as a blood pressure of 140/90 or greater. This refers to 140 mm Hg systolic and 90 mm Hg diastolic pressure. Systolic blood pressure is a measure of the pressure in the arteries when the heart beats. Diastolic pressure measures the pressure in the arteries between beats.

Cases where blood pressure is 130/80 should also be monitored carefully, as this could be a sign a person has a dramatic risk of developing hypertension. A blood pressure over 120/80 may be a concern to some patients.

Hypertension can develop over years and the patient may not experience any symptoms. Hypertension may be produced by underlying conditions. Such a concern is called secondary hypertension, and it may be triggered by kidney or thyroid problems, the use of some medications or illegal drug use.

Those with a family history of hypertension, older individuals, people with poor diets or physical routines and alcohol or tobacco users are at a higher risk. People who do not consume enough potassium and have too much sodium in their diet may also have a higher risk of developing hypertension. Excess stress may also cause the condition.

Some people with hypertension may experience headaches, shortness of breath or nosebleeds. However, most cases of hypertension are not identified until a dramatic heart-related event occurs.

If left untreated, hypertension can result in a heart attack or stroke, an aneurysm, heart failure, difficulties with memory and/or dementia.

An inflatable cuff placed over the arm is used to measure blood pressure. An ambulatory blood pressure measuring tool may also be provided for a patient to use over the course of 24 hours. This test can allow a medical professional to monitor the trends in how a person's blood pressure changes over the course of a day.

A patient with hypertension should be encouraged to:

1. Avoid consuming excess salt or sodium.
2. Exercise regularly and maintain a healthy weight.

3. Reduce alcohol consumption, possibly eliminating it if possible.

Thiazide diuretics may be prescribed to reduce the severity of the condition. Additionally, calcium channel blockers can relax the muscles in the blood vessels.

Hypotension

Hypotension (low blood pressure) occurs when blood pressure drops below 90/60.

A patient may experience dizziness or nausea. Fainting can also occur, as well as a general lack of concentration. If left untreated, hypotension may cause a person to go into shock.

Hypotension develops mainly among those who already have underlying heart concerns. It may be a sign of heart problems. An ECG or other exam is strongly encouraged.

Patients who are dehydrated or who have experienced blood loss may develop hypotension. Because the body's circulatory system expands dramatically during pregnancy, pregnant women may be prone to hypotension.

Some medications may also cause hypotension. Beta-blockers, alpha blockers, erectile dysfunction drugs and various drugs for the treatment of Parkinson's may affect blood pressure levels.

The following activities may trigger hypotension:

1. A person might develop low blood pressure after standing. This is known as postural hypotension.
2. Postprandial hypotension occurs when blood pressure drops after eating. People 65 years of age or older are at a greater risk of the concern.
3. Neurally mediated hypotension occurs when brain signals are not functioning correctly. As a result, the heart and brain are unable to communicate as well as they should, thereby impacting the heart's function.
4. Damage to the body's nervous system may also trigger hypotension.

A standard blood pressure test can help to diagnose hypotension. A tilt-table test may also be used, as it identifies how blood pressure may change based on when a person is sitting or lying down. An electrocardiogram should also be performed to assess whether the heart's general functionality is impacting blood pressure levels.

Patients with hypotension are encouraged to:

1. Consume more water, as water increases blood volume and prevents dehydration.
2. Wear compression stockings.
3. Add salt to their diets—with the caveat that this must be discussed and monitored by a doctor.

Fludrocortisone may be prescribed to improve blood volume, thus regulating blood pressure.

Peripheral Vascular Disease

Peripheral vascular disease (PVD) is a condition where the blood vessels outside the heart and brain experience damage. These vessels become narrow due to emboli or thrombi. Blood flow is therefore reduced and can cause significant damage if not swiftly treated.

Smokers and people whose veins have been affected by other medical conditions are at a higher risk for PVD.

Symptoms of PVD include cold feet or legs. Some aching and burning sensations may also be noted in the legs. These pains typically resolve when a person sits down.

The legs may lose color and become pale. Sores may develop around pressure points and may not heal properly.

An ankle-brachial index (ABI) measure may be used to assess the severity of the condition. The ABI is a measure of the systolic pressure at the ankle. The measure is divided by the systolic pressure at the arm.

A Doppler ultrasonography may also be used to assess peripheral arterial function.

A patient with PVD should be encouraged to exercise, eat healthily and refrain from smoking.

Anticoagulants or vasodilators should be part of treatment for PVD.

Cardiac Tamponade

Cardiac tamponade occurs when blood or fluid develops within the heart. The condition is more likely to develop in the pericardial sac or layer. As a result, the heart muscle becomes compressed due to the added fluid. The ventricles are unable to fill all the way, thus imposing additional stress on the muscle.

A patient may experience low blood pressure due to cardiac tamponade. Shortness of breath can also develop alongside general lightheadedness. The heart rate may also become faster, resulting in palpitations.

The fluid around the heart will need to be drained using a needle or tube inserted into the heart's tissue by a cardiologist. Cardiac tamponades may be fatal if not swiftly treated.

Cardiogenic Shock

Cardiogenic shock occurs when the heart is unable to pump enough blood to meet the body's needs. The condition may develop due to a heart attack or other forms of trauma. Myocarditis, endocarditis or any other inflammatory condition involving the heart may trigger the concern.

Older individuals are more likely to experience cardiogenic shock, as well as people with prior histories of heart disease.

Cardiogenic shock entails rapid breathing, tachycardia, hypotension, sweating, pallor and cold hands and feet. Pressure, pain around the chest and arms, shortness of breath and other signs associated with a heart attack may also develop.

Cardiogenic shock can be diagnosed through a blood pressure test. Hypotension often occurs among patients with shock. An ECG may be used to assess the heart's functionality. A chest X-ray can identify any excess fluid buildup in the lungs.

Inotropic agents like norepinephrine or dopamine may be administered as temporary solutions, prior to other treatments. Aspirin and antiplatelet medications can also be administered to reduce blood clotting. Some antiplatelet medications must be administered intravenously.

Surgery may be required in the most severe cases, when a patient is not responding to other treatment. A ventricular assistance device may be used to repair the heart and restore its pumping function. Some patients who use such a device may require a heart transplant later.

Deep Vein Thrombosis

Deep vein thrombosis (DVT) develops when a thrombus (a blood clot) forms. Typically, the clot forms in the leg, but it can also form in other parts of the body.

DVT causes swelling in the impacted area. In most cases, only one leg will be impacted, although there is a chance that swelling can occur in both legs at the same time. DVT causes pain in the leg, red or discolored skin and a warm feeling. Some people may have DVT for years before they notice any symptoms.

DVT can develop among people who have blood clotting disorders. People who have undergone extensive bed rest or paralysis may develop DVT as a result of lying still for long periods of time.

People who are overweight have a higher risk of developing DVT, as are pregnant women, as pressure will develop within the veins around the legs and pelvis.

A patient may potentially develop a PE due to DVT.

DVT can be diagnosed through an ultrasound. A venography can also be used, wherein dye is injected into a large vein to assess the location of the clot. An X-ray can determine exactly where the clot is.

Blood thinners may be prescribed. Thrombolytics, also known as clot busters, may also be used if the blood thinners aren't having the desired result. In severe cases, a vein filter can also be inserted into the vena cava vein in the abdomen to prevent a clot from breaking loose and entering the lungs, thereby forming a PE.

Compression stockings may help reduce the swelling involved with DVT.

Postphlebitic Syndrome

After DVT is treated, the affected vein might stop working as well as it should and postphlebitic or post-thrombotic syndrome may occur.

Inflammation can develop following DVT. The veins may become misshapen, and could struggle with carrying blood as they used to.

Symptoms of the syndrome include pain, itching and swelling in the leg or other areas where the thrombus develops. The skin may also become discolored. Some symptoms may progressively worsen.

An ultrasonography may help assess the inflammation caused by the condition.

Compression therapy is a necessary part of treatment and the patients' legs should be elevated. Proper wound care is necessary for any leg ulcers that may develop. Weight loss is a necessity for those who are overweight and experiencing significant pain.

Trauma Concerns

Types of Injuries

Various injuries may influence the cardiovascular system. These include dramatic forms of trauma that require appropriate treatment as soon as possible. The three main types of injuries are:

1. Penetrating – associated with gunshots, stabs or other things that suddenly enter the body
2. Blunt – trauma that injures a person but does not penetrate the body, such as blunt-force impact due to a car wreck
3. Medical – caused following the implantation of a medical device

Analysis Through the ABCDE System

The ABCDE system is used to assess the level of trauma. These are the steps that should be followed, in this order.

1. Airway

The airway should be assessed to ensure it's open and airflow is not obstructed.

2. Breathing

After the airway is secure, the patient's breathing should be assessed. The heart may be tested to compare its function to a patient's breathing. Proper ventilation may be required.

3. Circulation

The patient's circulation should be monitored including heart rate, blood pressure, body temperature and capillary refill time.

4. Disability

The person's ability to respond to stimuli should be addressed.

5. Exposure

Any clothing or other items interfering with a thorough examination should be removed. X-rays, CT scans and other intensive diagnostic processes may be recommended to further assess the extent of the injury.

Primary and Secondary Survey

After the patient has been stabilized, a primary survey should be performed which includes a full analysis of the trauma. A thorough assessment of the body, particularly at the site of the trauma, should be performed. The analysis confirms the situation at hand and should identify any problems that have the potential to develop, even if they are not currently present in a patient.

A secondary survey should be performed next. This includes a review of a patient's medications, allergies, illnesses, whatever the person's last meal might have been and any other pertinent information. The information should be used to assess a patient's current health and to help determine an appropriate treatment plan.

After the surveys are completed, physicians should be consulted about the treatment plan.

Chapter 6 – Diabetes

Topics pertaining to diabetes are combined in one segment of the exam alongside other conditions relating to the endocrine system and immunological concerns.

Treating diabetes requires regular monitoring to ensure the patient's blood sugar levels are kept in check. Diet is a key part of treatment.

The Basic Concept

Diabetes is a medical condition where the body is unable to produce insulin in response to blood glucose. The condition triggers hyperglycemia, which is an elevation of blood sugar levels.

Diabetes develops when the pancreas, which is responsible for the release of insulin, a hormone that regulates blood sugar levels, has impaired function.

The pancreas produces insulin in response to the glucose that one consumes. Glucose is a sugar responsible for facilitating many bodily functions including metabolic functions. Insulin is needed to allow glucose to be absorbed into the body's cells. A healthy individual will not have consistently high levels of glucose in his or her bloodstream.

Sometimes the pancreas produces insulin, but the body will not accept it. This keeps the glucose transferring accordingly.

Diabetes develops when the pancreas is unable to produce appropriate levels of insulin. Thus, insulin will not move the glucose to the cells, and it remains in the blood. The cells will not receive the glucose they need, making it harder for them to survive. Glucose is necessary for healthy cellular function. Hyperglycemia develops when cell function is impaired.

Blood testing should be used to assess a patient's blood sugar levels. Devices are available to allow people to test small samples of their blood at home. Even if a patient is not showing any symptoms of diabetes, he or she should test his or her blood regularly as blood sugar levels can fluctuate throughout the day.

Hyperglycemia

Blood sugar levels should normally be 70 to 130 mg/dL. Hyperglycemia occurs when blood sugar is at least 200 milligrams per deciliter or mg/dL. It's the most common problem seen in diabetic patients.

The symptoms of hyperglycemia are not likely to develop until blood sugar levels rise above 200. Not all people will show symptoms at this point, although a patient could potentially develop complications without being aware of the fact.

Hyperglycemia can occur due to a patient not getting enough insulin. Patients who consume more glucose than necessary or who do not take their medications correctly can be at risk. Stress may also be a factor in some patients.

Hyperglycemia causes symptoms such as polyuria, which is an increased desire to urinate, and polydipsia, which is an elevated thirst level.

Diabetic ketoacidosis may occur in some patients. The condition develops as the metabolic state impairs cell function. The patient may experience nausea and abdominal pain. A fruity breath may be noticeable. The metabolic imbalance may lead to a diabetic coma due to extremely elevated blood sugar levels.

Hypoglycemia

Hypoglycemia is the opposite of hyperglycemia. In this case, the patient's blood sugar is under 70 mg/dL. The condition occurs if the patient has an excess amount of insulin in the body. The condition develops in people with diabetes when they do not consume regular meals.

Hypoglycemia results in a reduced level of consciousness. Tremors, fatigue, sweating and fainting may occur, along with anxiety and blurry vision. Oral glucose is often prescribed to prevent the condition from worsening.

Types of Diabetes

Any of the following types of diabetes can result in hyperglycemia or hypoglycemia if the situation is not managed correctly.

Type 1 Diabetes

In type 1 diabetes, the pancreas is unable to produce insulin correctly. The condition is also referred to as juvenile diabetes, although it may develop at any age. The issue is triggered when the pancreas fails to fulfill its normal function.

Type 2 Diabetes

Type 2 diabetes is the most common form of diabetes. The body becomes insulin resistant, thus preventing it from using the insulin it requires. The pancreas can still produce insulin, but it will not reach the cells. The condition is common among those who are overweight.

Gestational Diabetes

Gestational diabetes develops in pregnant women, and the condition is temporary. The condition doesn't have many symptoms. A pregnant woman with gestational diabetes may be advised to eat a certain diet in order to help control the condition.

Monogenic Diabetes

Monogenic diabetes is inherited due to a gene mutation. In most cases, the body will be unable to produce enough insulin. In other cases, insulin resistance is the concern.

Prediabetes

Prediabetes does not necessarily mean that a patient has diabetes. The patient's blood glucose levels will be higher than usual. The totals are not high enough to make a proper diabetes diagnosis, but they are sufficiently elevated that a patient may have a higher risk of developing diabetes in the future.

General Symptoms

The symptoms of hyperglycemia and hypoglycemia include:

- Unexpected weight loss – may be due to frequent urination and because cells are not getting the energy they require as they are being deprived of glucose.
- Excess hunger – will develop even when the patient is eating a normal amount of food.
- Tingling hands and feet – the sensations develop due to nerve damage.
- Gum disease – the gums will retract from some people's teeth.
- Various wounds around the body may not heal correctly because the patient's immune system is impaired.

Testing

Standard Blood Test

A basic blood test can help assess blood glucose levels. The test, which requires only a single drop of blood, should take only a few seconds. A few tests should be performed while the patient is under observation. Multiple tests can confirm trends in a patient's blood sugar levels throughout the day or after meals.

General Screening

The following tests are recommended in order to screen for diabetes:

1. Fasting Blood Glucose Test

The fasting test, which involves taking blood right after a person first wakes up in the morning, assesses how the body is managing glucose levels. Prior to the test, the patient should not have had any food in the last eight hours or more. This is why the test is performed in the morning.

2. Oral Glucose Tolerance Test

The oral glucose tolerance test also requires a patient to fast for at least eight hours before the test. The patient then consumes eight ounces of a sugar compound. The person will take a second blood test about two hours after consuming the compound. This assesses how the patient's body handles glucose levels.

3. Hemoglobin A1C Test

An A1C test identifies the average glucose levels in a patient's blood over the past few months. The test involves no dietary restrictions. It should be administered multiple times over the course of a year.

A typical person's A1C level is from four to six percent. This means that the average daily blood glucose level should be around 100 to 120 mg/dL.

A patient with an A1C level over seven percent will be at risk of developing diabetes. A person with the condition should aim to keep his or her A1C total under that seven percent threshold.

Treatments

Medications

A patient may be prescribed medications depending on the severity of the diabetes. Insulin may help in some situations. Treatment often includes oral medications, although some injection-based medications may also be necessary.

DPP-4 inhibitors and GLP-1 receptor agonists may also be necessary, depending on an individual patient's needs.

Lifestyle Changes

Patients should be encouraged to make the appropriate lifestyle adjustments to improve their condition. These adjustments include:

1. Dietary changes

The patient should focus on a high-fiber diet while also reducing his or her sodium intake. The goal is for the patient to lose weight. A doctor may recommend that a patient visit a dietician to get professional advice on improving his or her diet to better manage his or her diabetes.

2. Avoiding alcohol if possible

Although a person doesn't necessarily have to completely stop drinking alcohol, excessive consumption may still increase the patient's risk of low blood sugar. There should be a limit of two drinks a day for a man or one drink a day for a woman. All sugary mixed drinks should be avoided, and the patient should also avoid drinking on an empty stomach.

3. Avoiding smoking

Smoking can increase the patient's risk of developing nerve damage, including in the eyes. Blood vessels that may already be weak due to diabetes can also be harmed. Patients should be encouraged to stop smoking completely in order to avoid future complications.

4. Exercise is also recommended, although it should be monitored by a doctor

Exercise can help a person lose weight, but it must be implemented under the supervision of a physician. A doctor will be able to determine how well the patient can handle various physical activities, and whether that person should avoid any possible risks associated with such activities. A stress test may help identify how well the patient is capable of responding to physical activity.

Treating An Emergency

In some cases, a patient with diabetes may experience an emergency. This may include cases where the patient has hyperglycemia and is at risk of falling into a diabetic coma.

Fluid replacement is recommended during an emergency. Intravenous fluids can help with restoring the fluids lost due to excessive urination. The fluids also dilute the excess sugar found in the blood.

Electrolytes, which can be lost due to a lack of insulin, may be replaced as necessary, to help restore the balance of blood sugar levels.

Insulin therapy can also work intravenously. The therapy process reverses the development of ketones in the blood.

Antibiotics can also be prescribed if a bacterial infection develops.

Glucose-Related Concerns

The following section focuses on conditions relating to diabetes that may develop due to the body's inability to handle glucose. This includes cases where glucose cannot be metabolized appropriately. While all forms of diabetes involve glucose-related concerns, the following issues are by-products of diabetes that can become particularly severe if not treated.

Diabetic Ketoacidosis

When the pancreas is unable to produce insulin, glucose will build up in the body. This excess of glucose causes ketoacids to be produced. This leads to diabetic ketoacidosis.

Diabetic ketoacidosis causes fatigue and general weakness. A person will also develop excessive thirst, abdominal pain, general shortness of breath and confusion. The effects may occur within 24 hours of the excess glucose building up.

A urine or blood test can be used to assess ketone levels and may be used to screen for hyperglycemia.

Diabetic ketoacidosis is more likely to occur among patients who are not following the prescribed insulin treatment. For example, a person may not consume enough insulin or could miss a treatment. Illnesses that trigger the production of cortisol or adrenaline may also be threats to a diabetic patient's well-being.

A blood test may be necessary for detecting ketoacidosis. A test can monitor for high blood sugar and ketone levels.

Fluid and electrolyte replacement are required for treatment purposes. Insulin therapy may also be necessary depending on the severity of the condition.

The patient should monitor his or her blood sugar multiple times a day to prevent ketoacidosis. Insulin dosages should also be checked as necessary.

Ketoacidosis should be carefully monitored even in patients who are not diabetic. There is a strong possibility the person might have diabetes, even if he or she has never been diagnosed.

Glycogenosis

Glycogenosis is a hereditary metabolic condition. Enzyme deficiencies in the body impact how glycogen is processed. In some cases, glycolysis will be impaired.

Growth issues may develop in a person who has glycogenosis. This is especially the case when it comes to children. Kidney stones and general confusion may also develop in some cases. If left untreated, the condition can cause intestinal sores and seizures. The condition may also lead to coma in the worst cases.

Carbohydrate consumption is critical for regulating the condition, in order to ensure blood sugar levels remain stable. Regular testing is necessary to monitor a patient's condition.

Metabolic Syndrome

A patient's risk of developing diabetes will increase if the person has metabolic syndrome, also known as syndrome X. Metabolic syndrome includes:

- Hypertension
- Hyperglycemia
- Excess body fat, particularly around the waist
- High cholesterol levels, including high triglyceride totals

People with metabolic syndrome are often overweight. The body will not produce insulin appropriately and blood sugar levels will rise as a result.

A person who does not exercise regularly or eat healthily has a greater risk of developing metabolic syndrome. Treatment should include a healthy diet and a regular exercise routine. A dietician may be consulted to help a person come up with a reasonable plan for eating healthily.

Chapter 7 – Endocrine System

The endocrine system assists in the production of hormones. Hormones support many functions in the body and therefore, impaired levels can significantly impact a person's well-being.

Critical Parts of the Endocrine System

The endocrine system includes the:

1. Hypothalamus

The hypothalamus links to the nervous system and tells the pituitary gland to either produce or stop generating hormones.

2. Pituitary Gland

The primary gland in the endocrine system, it takes in information from the brain and directly impacts how other glands operate. The pituitary gland produces human growth hormone, prolactin and luteinizing hormone.

3. Pineal Gland

The pineal gland produces melatonin, which helps regulate a person's sleep cycle.

4. Thyroid Gland

The thyroid produces a hormone that regulates the body's metabolic functions. The gland is necessary to keep a person's heart rate steady and burn fat.

5. Parathyroid

The parathyroid regulates calcium and phosphorus levels in the body.

6. Thymus

The thymus produces white blood cells or T-lymphocytes. The cells are critical for supporting a healthy immune system.

7. Adrenal Glands

The adrenal glands produce adrenaline and corticosteroids.

8. Pancreas

The pancreas produces digestive enzymes to break down foods and insulin to maintain blood sugar levels. The organ functions as a part of the digestive system.

9. Ovaries/Testes

The last part of the endocrine system varies by gender. The ovaries in women produce estrogen and progesterone. The testes in men produce testosterone. The hormones are critical to the onset of puberty.

Adrenal Concerns

Cushing's Syndrome

Cushing's syndrome occurs when the adrenal glands produce excess amounts of cortisol. A person may gain weight, bruise easily and develop weak bones and muscles. Some people with Cushing's syndrome might notice a slight hump on their back. Cushing's syndrome can also produce excess body hair, high blood pressure and changes in the skin's natural elasticity.

Medications that control the production of hormones in the body are necessary for treatment. Adrenal surgery is necessary in the most significant cases.

Addison's Disease

Addison's disease is a form of adrenal insufficiency. The adrenal glands are unable to produce the corticosteroids the body requires, including ones that manage fluid balances and electrolytes. As a result, a patient may develop fatigue and skin discoloration.

Steroid injections may be administered as one form of treatment. Surgery on the adrenal glands may be required if the steroid injections do not produce the desired results.

Conn's Syndrome

The adrenal glands may produce excess amounts of aldosterone due to Conn's syndrome. High blood pressure, muscle cramps and general fatigue and weakness can develop. Kidney disease may develop if the issue is not treated swiftly.

Tumors on the adrenal glands can cause Conn's syndrome. Surgery is necessary for removing these tumors. Such tumors are frequently benign, but will negatively influence the functionality of the glands. Some tumors may also be malignant and may become cancerous if not quickly removed.

A patient should avoid salt consumption to prevent the condition from becoming worse. Proper hydration is also key to preventing damage as a result of the condition.

Thyroid Concerns

For all conditions, thyroid levels may be monitored through a blood test. The test identifies the hormones produced, particularly thyroid-stimulating hormone (TSH). Antibody levels in the blood may also be monitored. An ultrasound may be necessary to monitor for tumors which could indicate a condition such as thyroid cancer.

Hyperthyroidism

Hyperthyroidism occurs when the thyroid gland produces an excess of thyroxine, a thyroid hormone. The condition accelerates the body's metabolic functions, thus promoting unintentional weight loss. Patients may experience an irregular heartbeat, arrhythmia, palpitations, tachycardia and heat sensitivity.

The added production of thyroxine may be triggered by Graves' disease, a condition where antibodies from the immune system stimulate the thyroid to produce excess hormones. The thyroid gland may become inflamed.

Radioactive iodine may help to shrink the thyroid if hormone production is too high.

Methimazole and other anti-thyroid medications may also be necessary for the treatment of the condition. Beta-blockers can help control thyroid levels.

A thyroidectomy may help in cases where the condition is not resolving on its own. This treatment is for people who do not respond well to anti-thyroid medications or who may not be comfortable receiving radioactive iodine. A majority of the thyroid gland is removed in the thyroidectomy process. After the surgery, levothyroxine will be necessary to help regulate thyroid hormone levels in the body. Medications to stabilize blood calcium levels may also be prescribed for some people. Such medications will be necessary for life, what with the thyroid gland no longer being present to help regulate natural functions.

The removal of the thyroid should be a last resort if the patient has not responded to any other forms of less invasive treatment.

Hypothyroidism

Hypothyroidism is the opposite of hyperthyroidism. In this case, the thyroid gland is not producing enough thyroid hormones, to the extent that the levels may not even be detectable in the blood.

A person with hypothyroidism may experience fatigue, constipation, muscle pains and a high blood cholesterol level. Some people may also experience thinning hair.

Hypothyroidism may develop in children. The condition will result in delayed puberty and a general lack of mental development.

Hypothyroidism may be triggered by thyroid surgery. Radiation therapy used for the treatment of various cancers may also weaken the gland. Lithium for the treatment of psychiatric disorders can also contribute to the development of the condition.

Daily treatment with levothyroxine is necessary for restoring the thyroid levels in the body. An annual review of TSH totals is necessary to ensure TSH levels are being regulated. A patient's needs for medication will vary and should be addressed on an individual level.

Goiter

A goiter is an enlarged thyroid gland. The gland can cause swelling in the neck area. It may feel tight and can produce coughing and hoarseness. The patient may not feel pain but could struggle to swallow or breathe correctly.

An iodine deficiency may trigger a goiter. Graves' disease or Hashimoto's disease may also be a factor. Those who have undergone radiation treatments for various cancers are at risk of developing a goiter.

A hormone test can be performed to assess thyroid hormone levels. In some cases, a goiter will not influence hormone production. An ultrasonography can also be used for diagnostic purposes.

It is best to wait and see if the thyroid is correctly producing hormones. The thyroid might go back to its original size after a while. But if the thyroid does not go back to its normal size, levothyroxine should be prescribed. This will help resolve hormone levels and can slow the release of thyroid hormone, thus reducing the size of the goiter. Surgery may be required to remove the gland in the worst cases, thus requiring lifetime levothyroxine treatment depending on the amount of the gland that was removed.

Hashimoto's Disease

Hashimoto's disease occurs when the thyroid is damaged by the immune system. Antibodies decide the thyroid is a foreign body and attack it accordingly.

Hashimoto's disease is more likely to develop among women, although men may also develop the condition. The illness most commonly occurs among middle-aged people.

A patient will experience fatigue, constipation, pallor and general muscle weakness. A person may develop a goiter or experience an increase in LDL cholesterol levels.

An antibody test may be performed as part of the diagnostic process.

Levothyroxine and other synthetic hormones should be prescribed to the patient. The hormone treatment can help with easing the goiter and the thyroid levels. An annual TSH review is necessary.

Pituitary Conditions

Issues pertaining to the pituitary gland may occur at any age though they are most likely to develop in children and adolescents. The following are pituitary conditions:

Gigantism

Acromegaly is a pituitary condition commonly referred to as gigantism. The pituitary gland produces an excess amount of growth hormone in adulthood. The bones grow in size, particularly in the hands, feet and face. A person may grow extremely tall while not building sufficient muscle tissue. This will result in weakened muscles and fatigue. Some facial features may also become enlarged. The excessive growth will cause intense pain, especially if the body's muscles are incapable of handling the rapid growth and added body mass. Fractures and other injuries may develop in some cases.

The situation may develop due to significant pituitary tumors. Some tumors may also develop in the lungs or pancreas. A CT scan may be necessary for diagnostic purposes.

A growth hormone suppression test may be performed to identify gigantism. The test entails measuring a patient's growth hormone totals before and after consuming a glucose compound. Glucose regularly reduces growth hormone levels. A patient with gigantism will continue to have a higher growth hormone total.

A surgical procedure is necessary to remove the tumors that trigger gigantism. A transsphenoidal surgery can be performed through the nose in order to access tumors in the brain. The procedure should normalize growth hormone production. Medications that reduce growth hormone production or dopamine agonists that limit hormone levels may help. Some radiation treatments may also be necessary in cases where some remaining cells from a tumor still exist.

Hypopituitarism

Hypopituitarism is a condition where the pituitary gland does not produce the levels of hormones the body needs, or fails to generate any at all. Fatigue, muscle weakness and body fat changes may occur. Some people may not feel motivated, what with the fatigue setting in.

Sexual changes may also develop. For men, there may be less facial or body hair, while erectile dysfunction may also develop in some patients. For women, hot flashes and a loss of pubic hair may occur. Some women may experience irregular periods, or even no periods.

Hypopituitarism may develop in adults as well as children. Even after the person is fully grown, human growth hormone is necessary for promoting energy and the development of muscle tissue. A malfunction in the pituitary gland may impair a person's energy levels and daily activities.

Hypopituitarism may occur due to a head injury or brain surgery. Radiation treatments in the area may also cause the condition. In rare cases, the immune system will produce a response that can weaken the body.

A blood test can detect cases of hypopituitarism. A CT scan of the brain may also help.

Corticosteroids may be prescribed, and growth hormones or sex hormones may also be utilized. A surgical procedure to remove any tumors that are causing the condition may also help. The treatment will vary based on the severity of the condition.

Chapter 8 – Immunological Conditions

Immunological conditions are situations where the body's immune system has become compromised, making it difficult for a patient to stay healthy. Patients with compromised immune systems may die even from minor illnesses due to their lack of normal bodily defenses.

SCID

Severe combined immunodeficiency (SCID) occurs at birth. The condition develops due to an impairment of the production of white blood cells. A child with an impaired immune system will not have enough lymphocytes to help protect his or her body. The existing lymphocytes may not function as well as they should. As a result, the child's immune system will not be able to protect him or her from viruses, fungi, bacteria and other external threats.

The condition occurs due to a malfunction on a gene on the X chromosome. A lack of an enzyme necessary for the production of lymphocytes may also trigger the disease.

A child with SCID may develop an infection such as pneumonia, meningitis or skin rashes. Regular diarrhea may occur, as well as oral thrush. The child may struggle to thrive and may experience significant breathing difficulties.

A blood test is necessary for diagnostic purposes and is best used on newborns to diagnose the condition as soon as possible.

A stem cell or bone marrow transplant is necessary for the treatment of SCID. The new cells from a donor will help rebuild a child's immune system. Cells from a family member are most compatible.

The time frame for treating SCID varies based on how well a child responds to treatment. During treatment, the child may be placed in isolation for a brief period to prevent infection while his or her immune system is recovering. During that time period, the child must be carefully monitored to ensure he or she is responding appropriately to treatment.

HIV

Human immunodeficiency virus (HIV) is a virus that directly affects the body's immune system.

The virus attacks CD4/T cells. Those cells are necessary for attacking bacteria, infections and other foreign bodies. Without them, a patient's health is severely compromised.

Transmission

HIV is transmitted through blood, sexual fluids and breast milk. It doesn't appear in saliva, urine, sweat or tears. The virus is spread by sharing infected needles or participating in sexual intercourse. HIV may also be spread from a mother to a child during birth.

The HIV virus is unable to last for long outside of the human body. Therefore, the virus cannot be spread by insects, animals or on communal surfaces such as toilet seats.

General Stages

HIV advances through specific stages. If untreated, it may develop into full-blown AIDS.

1. Acute Infection

An acute infection occurs as the patient develops the first symptoms of HIV, two to six weeks after first contracting the virus. During this stage, the patient may experience a headache, fatigue, muscle pains and a sore throat. The lymph nodes may also start to swell.

2. Chronic Infection

A chronic infection will result in regular flu-like symptoms. Not all people will notice these symptoms. A patient may experience this stage for ten years or longer. The infection involves HIV killing off the T cells necessary for protecting the immune system.

3. AIDS

If HIV is not treated during the two earlier stages, it will advance to full-blown AIDS. AIDS is fatal if not appropriately treated.

Testing and Screening

While testing a person for AIDS, he or she should be asked the following information on his/her personal history:

- Has he/she engaged in unprotected sex, particularly with someone he/she does not know?
- How many sexual partners has he/she had recently?
- Has he/she had sex for drugs or money?

- Has he/she injected drugs in the past? If so, details should be asked about the types of drugs, whether or not needles were ever shared, time frame, etc.
- Has he/she ever been diagnosed with hepatis or an STD?
- Has he/she ever been sexually assaulted?

The testing process takes several weeks and involves the following steps:

1. Blood is drawn from the patient in order to study the antibodies produced.
2. Two to eight weeks later, an antibody test is performed.
3. An antigen test will identify the p24 protein. The protein can appear about a month after the infection develops. HIV antibodies may also appear in the body at this point.

A positive test indicates the presence of HIV. An antibody differential test or Western blot test will then be necessary. A secondary test should also be taken in a few months to confirm the original results. If HIV is indeed present in the blood, antibodies will be much more visible at that point.

Viral Load Testing

A viral load test may identify the condition in some patients. The test assesses how well the body is handling RNA, a part of HIV that helps the virus reproduce. A test can identify multiple copies of the RNA in a milliliter of blood.

A viral load may identify a high load of 100,000 copies or more. A high load indicates the virus is progressing fast. Less than 10,000 copies indicates that the virus is present, but it is not reproducing as quickly as expected. Proper treatment is required to ensure the viral load is kept in check and that the virus is not likely to spread any further.

Treatment

HIV treatment entails daily antiretroviral therapy (ART). ART treatment should begin as soon as the person is diagnosed with HIV. Such drugs will help to reduce the copies of the virus in the blood, thus preventing HIV from developing into AIDS.

Types of HIV Drugs

Each patient's treatment must be individualized based on his or her needs. The following are the various medications available for HIV treatment:

1. NRTIs

Nucleoside/nucleotide reverse transcriptase inhibitors prompt the virus to produce impaired building blocks. The infected cells are then unable to reproduce or further spread the virus.

2. NNRTIs

Non-nucleoside reverse transcriptase inhibitors bind to proteins within the body, keeping the HIV from producing copies of itself off these proteins.

3. Protease Inhibitors

Such drugs block proteins that infected cells would otherwise use to produce new HIV particles.

4. INSTIs

Integrase inhibitors, also known as integrase strand transfer inhibitors, stop HIV from reproducing by blocking a protein that would move the virus DNA into the DNA of another healthy cell.

5. Fusion Inhibitors

A fusion inhibitor prevents HIV from entering healthy cells. The inhibitor is different from other drugs that target infected cells. Its goal is to ensure an existing cell is not at risk of possible harm.

6. CCR5 Antagonist

A CCR5 antagonist blocks outside ports that might allow the virus to enter and thrive in health cells. The goal is to keep the virus from using certain entry points in the cells in order to spread.

7. Post-Attachment Inhibitor

A post-attachment inhibitor blocks HIV-infected cells from harming healthy cells. The drug is administered intravenously. The treatment is relatively new, so there are no guarantees that all hospitals or medical facilities have access to such treatments. The treatment is recommended for those who have aggressive forms of the virus that might not respond as well to other treatments.

Many of these medications can be combined without possible reactions, although consistent monitoring and adjusting of the treatment as needed is vital.

AIDS

HIV must be treated as soon as possible. If left unchecked, the virus will damage the immune system to the point where it cannot be restored.

When a patient reaches the point of having fewer than 200 T cells per cubic millimeter of blood, the person is diagnosed as having AIDS. AIDS leads to various chronic diseases. Ultimately, the disease severely compromises the body's immune system so even minor illnesses can kill a person.

Signs of AIDS

One key sign of AIDS is Kaposi's sarcoma, a type of skin cancer that is prominent in people with the disease. Pneumonia may also be present, especially stronger, recurring forms.

In addition to the symptoms of HIV, a person with AIDS may also develop swollen lymph nodes, unusual weight loss that cannot be controlled, severe diarrhea, yeast infections in varying parts of the body and unexplained bruises or bleeding.

Unless treated appropriately, a person who is diagnosed with AIDS will often die one to three years after the initial diagnosis. Nowadays, many treatments are available which did not exist when HIV was first discovered, so life expectancy is significantly better for those who receive prompt, consistent treatment.

Vaccination Considerations for HIV and AIDS

Patients who have HIV or AIDS are encouraged to get regular vaccinations to prevent infections. They also require an annual flu vaccination to prevent the virus from spreading.

A vaccine should be inactivated, meaning that it does not have any living germs. A living germ in a vaccine may cause a mild form of a disease in a patient with HIV. That risk becomes more significant among those with AIDS.

Specific Vaccinations

The following vaccinations should be administered to people who have HIV or AIDS to protect them from possible harm:

- Influenza (every year)
- Hepatitis B
- Measles, mumps and rubella (only if T cell count is over 200)

- Pneumonia (every five years)
- Tetanus (every 10 years)
- PPSV23
- PCV13 (as soon as HIV diagnosis is made)
- HPV (if under the age of 26; pregnant women should not receive the vaccination)
- Bacterial meningitis (two separate vaccinations in two months)

Risks to Note

A vaccine may increase a patient's viral load. The patient should not have any infections or other illnesses when receiving a vaccine. This is because the vaccine could worsen underlying conditions.

A T cell count test may be required before a person receives a vaccination. This is because a vaccine may not be effective if the T cell count is too low.

HIV or AIDS patients should avoid people who have had live vaccines in the past few weeks such as the chicken pox, MMR or flu vaccines.

Chapter 9 – Confusion-Related Concerns

There may be cases where a person who has been in a hospital or other medical facility for a prolonged period develops sudden confusion. In many cases, the issue may be an underlying issue related to a prior condition.

Delirium

Delirium is a sudden form of confusion. It can develop in a few hours, although it may also progress over a few days while a person is hospitalized.

Delirium causes a person to become unable to focus. For example, the patient may not be able to stick to certain topics or thoughts. Sometimes that person might become overly fixated upon certain details without any real reason.

Cognitive impairment may develop due to confusion. A person's memory may suffer. He or she may become disoriented in terms of location or personal identity.

Hallucinations may occur as the patient starts to see things that do not exist. The person may become agitated, increasingly frustrated or withdrawn.

Other patients may experience hypoactive delirium, feeling unusually fatigued.

Delirium may develop due to a person suddenly being sent to a medical facility during an emergency. The patient may become disoriented and incapable of fully processing what is happening. In other cases, drugs or alcohol may directly contribute to the issue. Some infections and other conditions may also cause the rapid onset or deterioration of the condition.

Appropriate emotional help is necessary for controlling the patient's delirium. He or she should be kept in a quiet, peaceful environment in order to mitigate anxiety. Lighting should be comfortable and appropriate to the time of day. Any medications a person is taking should be monitored, as there is a chance some of these medications might trigger cases of delirium.

Dementia

Dementia is a condition where the patient loses control of his or her cognitive functions. While delirium is temporary, dementia is permanent.

A person who experiences dementia will suffer from memory loss and have trouble communicating. He or she may struggle to reason or use logic and will have difficulty planning and organizing activities. Dementia patients may suffer from anxiety, agitation, depression and/or hallucinations.

Patients with Alzheimer's disease, Huntington's disease or who have experienced traumatic brain injuries in the past may be at a higher risk of developing dementia.

Patients with dementia should be carefully monitored for signs of the disease's progression and other infections, illnesses, etc. Thiamin, copper and vitamin E levels should also be monitored in order to prevent nutritional deficiencies which could worsen the condition.

To assist with diagnosis, a CT scan or MRI may be used to examine a person's brain. A cognitive test may also be used to assess a patient's orientation, judgment and other critical reasoning skills.

Dementia does not have a cure, but it can be controlled to some extent. Cholinesterase inhibitors may be prescribed to reduce the severity of the condition. Memantine may also be prescribed to enhance brain function and to support communication between nerve cells.

Chapter 10 – Chemotherapy

Chemotherapy is a process that entails the use of drugs to treat various cancers.

Chemotherapy is designed to target the entire body, including in cases where cancers might have spread throughout. The goal is to get a patient into remission, to the point where it's unlikely the cancer will return:

Various things may happen in the chemotherapy process:

- Cancer cells may be inhibited so they don't divide and spread.
- Any sources of energy that the cancer cells require may be inhibited. These include hormones or enzymes which are necessary for cells' growth.
- Apoptosis may be triggered as the cancer cells kill themselves off.
- The growth of blood vessels that support the tumor may also be inhibited.
- The size of a tumor may shrink before a surgical procedure.
- Patients may still receive chemotherapy after surgery or during remission to remove any remaining cancer cells.

The effectiveness of chemotherapy will vary based on the condition that the patient has. In the earliest stages of cancer, chemotherapy will help prevent cancer from spreading and may reduce cancerous growths. In later stages of the disease, the treatment will help relieve the patient's pain and other symptoms, although it may be too late to remove the cancer altogether. The general prognosis for survival during a later stage of cancer is poor. The earlier a cancer patient receives chemotherapy, the better.

The amount of time a chemotherapy treatment lasts will vary based on the type of cancer and its severity. Some cancers require weeks of treatment. Others require only a few days.

A rest period is necessary if the patient requires multiple treatments. This rest period could be anywhere from one to three weeks. The rest is necessary to prevent a patient from becoming unduly fatigued, which is one of chemotherapy's frequent side effects.

Blood Testing

A blood test is necessary to assess how well a patient will cope with chemotherapy. The test should include an analysis of red and white blood cell counts and platelet counts. Individuals with low blood counts must wait for these to improve before undergoing chemotherapy. Medications to support the development of new blood cells and platelets may be prescribed.

Liver Testing

A liver function test (along with a blood test) may also be required in order to assess how a patient will handle chemotherapy. This is because the liver breaks down chemotherapy drugs. If a patient has a diseased liver, it will struggle to fulfill its function when taxed by the chemotherapy medications. Chemotherapy may need to be postponed until a person's liver is healthy enough to handle the treatment.

Administration

Chemotherapy is administered in one of three forms:

1. Orally, through tablets or liquids
2. Intravenously
3. Topically, often through a lotion or a patch

Some chemotherapy can be administered at home. Other treatments require hospitalization. Once begun, no treatments can be missed. Any patient who misses a dose of chemotherapy drugs should consult a doctor immediately. It's vital that the treatment is carefully monitored.

Types of Chemotherapy Drugs

The following are types of chemotherapy drugs, administered depending on the type of cancer and severity of the condition.

1. Alkylating Agents

Alkylating agents influence the DNA of cancer cells. The drugs kill off the cells and are most effective when the cells reach certain stages.

2. Antimetabolites

An antimetabolite imitates the proteins that cells require for their survival. The cancer cells consume these proteins, but they do not include the components needed for survival. Therefore, the cancer cells starve and die off.

3. Plant Alkaloids

Plant alkaloids inhibit cellular growth. When cells do grow or divide, it's easier for other drugs to kill them off.

4. Antitumor Antibiotics

Antibiotic medications can stop cells in tumors from growing. These antibiotics are different from medications used for controlling infections.

All drugs help control the development of cancers and can even lead to full remission, but they also harm healthy cells. Patients must be monitored for their responses to various treatments.

These drugs may also be paired with other cancer treatments, including surgical procedures.

Side Effects

While effective in treating cancer, chemotherapy has many negative side effects because it targets both healthy and diseased cells. Most side effects go away after the treatment ends.

Side effects may include:

- General nausea and vomiting
- Hair loss
- Skin pallor
- Fatigue
- Damage to the nervous system; this includes temporary hearing loss
- Infections; this is due to the white blood cell count dropping
- Bleeding; the drop in the body's platelet total is a factor
- Anemia triggered by a loss of red blood cells
- Lack of appetite
- Diarrhea or constipation triggered by the body purging damaged cells
- Cognitive issues; this may be due to the medications' temporary influence on the nervous system

Chapter 11 – Genitourinary Issues

Foreign Body

A foreign body may develop in the male urological system, especially when a catheter has been used. A CT scan or other outside scan may be necessary for identifying where the foreign body is located.

An endoscope may be used to remove the foreign body. If an endoscope isn't effective, a suprapubic cystectomy procedure may also be required. The area should be monitored after the foreign body is removed to ensure sepsis does not develop.

Infection

An infection in the genitourinary (GU) tract may involve bacteria influencing the general health of the GU tract. The prostate gland, testes, kidneys, urethra or bladder may develop inflammation.

An infection is often triggered by the introduction of a catheter. In other cases, unprotected sex may be a factor.

A patient with an infection will experience pain when urinating. A fever, pain in the pubic area and penile discharge may also develop. The scrotal area may be extremely tender.

A CT scan may be performed for diagnostic purposes. An IV pyelogram may also be used.

An antimicrobial treatment is necessary for preventing the infection from spreading or growing. Analgesics may also be administered. The kidneys should be monitored in the treatment process to ensure they are not damaged.

Priapism

Priapism is a condition where the penis is erect for an extended period of time. The condition is often caused by a lack of blood flow out from the penile tissue, although trauma to the GU tract may also trigger the condition.

Priapism may be caused by the use of medications for the treatment of erectile dysfunction. Sickle cell disease, dialysis, various cancers of the GU tract and heparin use may also be factors. Injuries to the penile tissue may cause the development of priapism in some patients.

The fluid in the corpora cavernosa should be removed as soon as possible to prevent complications. Saline irrigation may also be administered to ease the area.

Phenylephrine may be administered as a vasoconstrictive agent. The compound should be applied every five minutes until the issue is resolved.

A shunt may be inserted between the corpora cavernosa and the glans penis. Any bleeding should be swiftly stopped. The erection should disappear during the treatment process.

Renal Calculi

A renal calculus, also known as nephrolithiasis or a kidney stone, is a compound that forms in the kidney. The condition causes pain when a person tries to urinate. Such pain can become more significant when a stone calculus exits the kidney.

The condition causes sharp, sudden pain in the abdomen. Blood may also appear in the patient's urine.

A calculus is mainly composed of calcium. Uric acid and struvite may also be present. Some of these stones may form due to antacid consumption. People who suffer from insulin resistance may also be at higher risk of developing the condition.

A kidney function test can help identify the condition. A CT scan may also identify any specific locations where renal calculi may occur.

Regular pain relievers should be prescribed to ease a patient's discomfort. The patient should be advised to drink more water to help with passing the stone. Added water may help with weakening the stone, thus making it easier for the calculus to pass through the body.

External shockwave therapy may be necessary to break up larger stones.

Testicular Torsion

Torsion occurs when a testicle rotates and the cord that supplies blood to the scrotum underneath becomes twisted. The issue may develop due to an injury in the area, often caused by intense physical activity. In rare cases, the issue may develop while the patient is asleep.

The condition can cause a permanent reduction in a man's fertility if not rapidly treated. Intense pain can lead to swelling in some cases.

A surgical procedure is necessary to save the testicle and preserve the patient's fertility. A Doppler image can assess how the testicle is positioned once it is moved into the scrotum.

The Testicular Workup for Ischemic and Suspected Torsion (TWIST) score assesses:

- Swelling in the area
- A hard testicle
- Lack of a reflex in the area
- High-riding testicle
- Whether the patient is vomiting or experiencing nausea

The more of these signs a patient has, the higher the score. A high score suggests a higher risk of torsion, requiring immediate treatment.

Urinary Retention

Urinary retention occurs when a patient has difficulty urinating because the bladder is not emptying fully when the person voids. The condition occurs mainly among men, although it can also develop in some women. The issue is also more common among older people.

Urinary retention can be caused by an enlarged prostate, or by a disease such as diabetes. Anticholinergic medications may also trigger the condition.

Patients who have kidney or bladder stones may be at a higher risk of developing urinary retention issues, as are individuals who have experienced a prior injury or trauma to the area.

A traditional physical exam may be required, along with a full personal history.

A patient may need to perform self-catheterization. The process entails threading a catheter into the urinary tract to help empty the bladder as necessary.

The patient should be advised to regulate his or her fluid consumption and diet to prevent the condition from worsening. Kegel exercises and other forms of physical therapy may help improve a patient's bladder function. Some medications may also be prescribed, although such treatments may not be effective and could cause accidental urination in the worst cases.

In some cases, a tumor may be present and have to be removed. Surgery may be required to divert urine if a patient's condition doesn't improve following traditional treatment.

Chapter 12 – Gynecological Concerns

Vaginal Bleeding

Vaginal bleeding can occur when a woman is menstruating, pregnant or experiencing a systemic illness. But there may also be other cases where vaginal bleeding occurs.

Unusual bleeding episodes may be triggered by:

- Sores that develop in the genital area
- Menopause due to hormonal changes in the body
- Anticoagulant drug use
- Trauma in many forms, including harm to the vaginal wall
- Cancerous conditions

A Pap smear, hormonal assay or CBC test may help with identifying any possible concerns. A CT scan may also help diagnose cancer. Liver and thyroid function may be tested.

A pelvic ultrasonography is strongly recommended to identify any cancerous bodies.

Any pathologies that trigger vaginal bleeding must be treated. Oral contraceptives that prevent the endometrial lining from thickening may be prescribed. Patients should be advised to remain properly hydrated, to enhance their recovery.

Foreign Body

A foreign body may appear in the vaginal tissue due to tampons, condoms and other items. The condition is more common in younger people.

The foreign body may penetrate the vaginal wall and cause intense pain and discomfort. Bleeding can develop in severe cases. Pain can spread to the abdomen and back.

A full exam is necessary for identifying the concern. A CT scan or ultrasonogram can help to locate the foreign body.

In most cases, an endoscope, introduced through the vagina, may be used to remove the foreign body. A more detailed surgical procedure may be required if there is an infection or other significant concern. At all times, bleeding must be controlled.

Gynecologic Hemorrhage

A gynecologic hemorrhage involves severe bleeding from the vagina. The bleeding can occur in between regular menstrual periods. Postcoital bleeding can also develop in between sexual activities.

The hemorrhage may continue for several days and could cause intense pain.

Hormonal changes might cause the hemorrhage. Women who have experienced trauma in the area may be at higher risk. An ovarian cyst may also be the cause of the problem.

A complete blood count is necessary to determine whether the hemorrhage has caused anemia. A pregnancy test should also be performed.

Hormonal therapy should help, or dilation and curettage may also be performed. A laparoscopic procedure may be performed in cases where the condition isn't responding to other types of treatment.

Vaginal Yeast Infection

A vaginal infection, officially referred to as candida vulvovaginitis, involves an overgrowth of yeast in the vagina. The infection produces irritation around the vulva and the vaginal area. A discharge or intense itchiness may develop in some cases. Redness and swelling may also occur.

If a patient suffers from four or more infections in a year, she is said to have a complicated yeast infection. The issue may also develop if a woman is pregnant, has uncontrolled diabetes or has another underlying condition such as HIV.

Yeast is necessary to control the development of healthy bacteria in the region. However, the candida yeast may grow too fast, thus moving the yeast into the deeper vaginal cell layers. The issue may be triggered by the use of antibiotics, pregnancy, a compromised immune system or the use of oral contraceptives that can increase estrogen levels.

A pelvic exam should be performed, utilizing a speculum to allow the vagina and cervix to be thoroughly examined. Any secretions should be gathered and tested for infection.

A single dosage of fluconazole may be necessary, although it's not appropriate for pregnant women. Two separate dosages may be required, taken a few days apart. Antifungal medications may also be prescribed for about a week to resolve the condition.

A boric acid capsule may be inserted in the vaginal area to treat bacteria that has been resistant to other medications. Boric acid capsules should not be orally consumed, as the compound can be deadly if digested.

A woman with a yeast infection should be encouraged to avoid hot tubs or baths, antibiotics for reasons other than colds or infections, and wet surfaces. Women should be advised not to douche, as the process removes healthy bacteria that protects the vaginal area from infection.

Ovarian Cyst

An ovarian cyst is a mass that appears on the ovary's surface. The cyst may be solid or filled with fluid.

An ovarian cyst will often be harmless and can go away on its own in a few months. But some cysts may rupture and cause intense pain, causing vomiting, fever and other complications. A pelvic exam will be necessary for diagnosis and to determine how to treat the condition.

Ovarian torsion may occur in cases where the cyst becomes too large. Torsion can inhibit blood flow to the area. Long-term effects of torsion can include a permanent loss in sexual function.

A pelvic exam can identify the specific type of ovarian cyst. A dermoid cyst may develop in some situations, featuring skin or teeth. Such a cyst grows from embryonic cells. Cystadenomas may also develop on an ovary and include a watery compound on the inside. Endometriomas may grow due to uterine endometrial cells growing outside of the uterus, thus producing growths that link to the ovary. All of these cysts can cause an ovary to shift out of place and thereby cause intense pain.

In addition to a pelvic exam, a patient's medical history should also be examined. A pregnancy test is also important to ensure the pain isn't pregnancy related.

Oral contraceptives are often prescribed for the treatment of cysts. A laparoscopy may be required in cases where the cyst is too large for conventional treatment to be effective.

Managing Cases of Sexual Assault

Sometimes a female patient will report that she has been sexually assaulted or raped. Such instances may include:

- Blood or sperm appearing in or on the woman's body. This is assuming she has not tried to clean herself off.

- Contusions and other forms of trauma may be noted.
- Any instance of vaginal penetration should be noted, including any discharge
- Abdominal trauma may develop.
- Lacerations may be visible.

The treatment process involves attending to any injuries the woman has. These include any potentially life-threatening concerns.

The patient must be tested for any sexually transmitted diseases. Antibiotics may be prescribed, along with other medications as necessary.

An appropriate psychological intervention should also be planned to help a woman cope with the ordeal she has been through, including post-traumatic stress disorder.

The patient should be interviewed about what happened during the assault. Although the patient might be reluctant to discuss what happened, it is critical for her to provide as many details as possible.

All documentation should be recorded responsibly to ensure that the patient's rights are protected. She must be provided the opportunity for confidentiality and privacy. If a woman, in her distress, is threatening self-harm, the appropriate professionals should be quickly advised so as to provide her with the right care and support.

A woman should be referred to a separate gynecologist after her initial treatment is complete. The gynecologist can monitor for complications following the assault and can continue to support the woman with any necessary ongoing treatment.

Chapter 13 – Obstetrical Health Considerations

Obstetrics refers to the efforts involved in childbirth and in helping a woman to give birth. Obstetrics is in the urological segment of the exam, as it focuses on a critical aspect of reproduction and female urology.

The following chapter concentrates on some of the complications that may develop during pregnancy. Some of these points entail the birthing process and what the woman will experience after giving birth.

During the Pregnancy

Placental Abruption

Placental abruption occurs when the placenta detaches from the uterus. This impacts the fetus' ability to receive blood and oxygen. The mother may also experience intense internal bleeding.

Placental abruptions occur during the third trimester. Vaginal bleed, abdominal pain and tenderness in the uterus are common. Consistent uterine contractions may be felt.

A woman who experiences hypertension has a high risk of having an abruption. A fall or other form of pressure to the abdomen may also be a concern. Women who are 40 years of age or older are also at a greater risk of developing the condition.

Blood clotting issues may develop in some cases. This may result in the mother needing a transfusion. CBC and coagulation tests are recommended for diagnostic purposes.

While an ultrasound may help with monitoring the unborn child, it may not detect the abruption.

After 34 weeks of pregnancy, it may be best to deliver the baby as soon as a placental abruption is detected. A C-section may be necessary, alongside a blood transfusion.

Ectopic Pregnancy

An ectopic pregnancy occurs when the fertilized ovum appears in the fallopian tube or another site away from the uterus. The ovum will be unable to develop, as it will not receive any blood and nutrients. This ectopic growth can become life-threatening.

An ectopic pregnancy is caused by a malfunction in the fallopian tubes. A woman who uses intrauterine devices or smokes has a higher risk of developing the condition. This is because smoking can inhibit the fallopian tubes' motility.

Vaginal bleeding can occur due to an ectopic pregnancy. A woman may also experience severe pain in the region and/or feel excessively weak or fatigued.

A BHCG test should be performed to confirm the ectopic pregnancy. The test requires a urine sample.

A laparoscopy is often recommended for the removal of the pregnancy. Intramuscular methotrexate may also be prescribed, although a liver and kidney test should be performed first, to assess a woman's overall ability to respond well to the medication.

Hyperemesis Gravidarum

Hyperemesis gravidarum (HG) is a form of nausea that develops during pregnancy. While pregnant women often experience "morning sickness," there may be times when nausea becomes severe. Regular vomiting may result in dehydration. The woman may become faint when standing.

A urinalysis test of the acid-base balance in a woman's body will help to identify the condition. A liver function test may help to rule out hepatitis as a factor. An ultrasound should be performed to assess the health of the fetus.

Ketosis may be a factor in HG and electrolytes can help keep a woman hydrated and ease her discomfort.

The Delivery Process

Emergent Delivery

An emergent delivery occurs when a baby is delivered after regular contractions start abruptly. The birthing process begins without warning. The labor process is brief and may require extra care.

In most cases, a woman may be in labor for about 12 to 24 hours before giving birth. This time frame is especially true for first-time mothers. A mother who experiences labor for about four hours or less is said to have an emergent delivery. This time may be even shorter for a woman who has given birth in the past.

A nurse must determine if the baby should be delivered in the emergency room or at the appropriate obstetrical department in a hospital facility.

Apgar Testing

The Apgar test should be performed about one to five minutes after the baby is delivered. The test assesses:

1. Appearance

The baby's skin color should be assessed. The baby should have a pinkish appearance with no cyanosis. Cases where a baby's body is blue or pale, or instances where the body is pink but the extremities are blue, should be noted immediately.

2. Pulse

The pulse should be at least 100 beats per minute. A pulse under this number may be a cause for concern.

3. Grimace

A child's irritability reflex should be measured. This means the baby should cry or pull away when stimulated. Any cases where the baby does not respond or has a very minimal response should be recorded.

4. Activity

The activity measurement involves an assessment of the baby's muscle tone. There might be times when the baby is not flexing too much, and that's okay, but there should be some semblance of movement.

5. Respiration

The baby should have a strong cry and be capable of breathing alone. There might be times when the baby is gasping or otherwise struggling for air. This could indicate an issue with his or her airway.

All Apgar test information should be carefully recorded. Emergency care may be required for babies who don't score well on the test.

Hemorrhage

A woman may lose a significant amount of blood during the birthing process. A hemorrhage involves a loss of 500 ml of blood or more during a vaginal delivery or 1000 ml or more during a C-section. The blood loss may be due to intense trauma in the birthing process or due to an extended labor. A hemorrhage may also develop during a multiple birth.

A surgeon should be consulted if a hemorrhage occurs in the birthing process. About six units of red blood cells should be prepared for transfusion depending on the amount of blood loss the woman experiences. Electrolytes should be administered.

A woman's uterus and vagina should be examined after she gives birth. Surgery may be required to correct the hemorrhage.

Chapter 14 – Neurological, Musculoskeletal and Integumentary Health

The last of the domains in the exam focuses on conditions that relate to the brain, muscles, skin and other tissues that protect the body.

Stroke

A stroke, which occurs when brain tissues die off due to an injury, is a significant threat to the patient's neurological health.

General Signs

Some of the common signs of a stroke include trouble speaking or understanding words, paralysis in the face or another part of the body. The patient may also experience vision difficulties in one or both eyes. A patient may also experience a sudden loss of coordination that makes walking difficult.

The symptoms become exacerbated if the stroke isn't swiftly treated. Failure to provide rapid treatment will result in the death of brain tissue. Providing medical attention to a patient as quickly as possible is absolutely critical.

The FAST Analysis

The FAST analysis may be used to identify the signs of a stroke:

1. Face – A part of the patient's face may start to droop.
2. Arms – The patient should be asked to raise his or her arms. During a stroke, one arm might drift in one direction or be unable to be raised.
3. Speech – Speech may be slurred or otherwise incoherent.
4. Time – Emergency treatment should be administered immediately if any of the above signs are noted. Time is critical, as the effects of the stroke will worsen if it is not treated fast.

Ischemic Stroke

An ischemic stroke is the most common stroke that a patient may experience. An ischemic stroke entails a blood clot developing in the brain, preventing blood from moving through the brain's blood vessels. The lack of blood causes brain cells to die off. This can cause irreversible brain damage and may be fatal if not rapidly treated

Hypoxia develops in the brain due to an ischemic stroke. ATP stores are lost. Cytotoxic edema may also occur due to excess water entering the brain cells.

An ischemic stroke may take one of two forms:

1. In a thrombotic stroke, a thrombus will develop in an artery that moves blood into the brain. Plaque may build up in the brain, thus keeping blood from flowing.
2. The other form of an ischemic stroke is an embolic stroke. A blood clot will develop in the heart or another part of the brain. The clot moves through the bloodstream and eventually enters the narrower arteries around the body. An embolus will form as the blood clots in the brain area.

A patient is more likely to experience an ischemic stroke due to being overweight, inactive or consuming excess alcohol. People who use cocaine and other illegal drugs have a greater risk of a stroke. Hypertension and high cholesterol also raise the risk of ischemic strokes. There is also a potential that a stroke may be a hereditary issue due to a gene mutation that may trigger the development of cholesterol in the body, although further research is required to confirm this.

Part of treatment involves stabilizing the patient. Alteplase is the only fibrinolytic agent that can treat an ischemic stroke. Antiplatelet agents should be administered to prevent further clots from developing. A thrombectomy may also be required if other treatments are not working.

The patient should be monitored for hyperthermia, hypertension or cardiac arrest, all of which may develop due to the shock produced by the stroke.

Hemorrhagic Stroke

A hemorrhagic stroke is a less common stroke that occurs when a vessel in the brain leaks or ruptures. It may be caused by hypertension, an aneurysm or the excessive use of anticoagulants for various medical treatments.

A hemorrhagic stroke may be an intracerebral or subarachnoid hemorrhage. An intracerebral hemorrhage occurs when a blood vessel bursts and spills into the brain tissues around the area, damaging brain cells. It may be caused by hypertension or anticoagulant use.

A subarachnoid hemorrhage occurs when an artery on or near the brain's surface bursts and leaks into the area between the brain's surface and the skull. The bleeding may be accompanied by a headache. The blood vessels may widen due to the injury, preventing blood flow.

A complete blood count may be used for diagnostic purposes. A coagulation study may also help determine the severity of the stroke. FAST may also be used to assess a patient.

A CT scan or MRI may be used to assess brain damage. A patient's hypertension may need to be treated as part of the medical intervention for the stroke. ACE inhibitors and beta-blockers can help with controlling the bleeding and easing the stress. The goal should be to reduce the systolic blood pressure to under 140 mm Hg.

Diuretic therapy may be used to treat the stroke. A patient's head should be elevated during treatment. Steroid therapy is not recommended as it has been proven ineffective.

The potential for a person to recover from a hemorrhagic stroke is not as strong as it is for an ischemic stroke. The mortality rate within 30 days of the event is high, especially among those who take warfarin. Vitamin K may be administered intravenously to reduce the patient's risk of death, although results will vary.

Transient Ischemic Attack

A transient ischemic attack (TIA), also known as a mini stroke, is a temporary form of a stroke. The symptoms the patient experiences are similar to what one might experience in a traditional stroke. The brain will temporarily lose part of its blood supply, thus triggering stroke-like symptoms. A TIA only lasts for a few minutes on average.

The TIA occurs due to a clot being formed in the nervous system. Although the effects are temporary and will not cause permanent effects, a TIA may put a person at higher risk of developing an actual stroke in the future. Indeed, a person may have a stroke as soon as a few days after the TIA episode. The TIA may be a sign of a patient having a narrowed artery or blood clot. The patient should still receive immediate medical attention, as there is always the possibility that a real stroke may be misinterpreted as a TIA by accident.

The patient should be treated for the TIA with anticoagulants or antiplatelet drugs. Thrombolytic agents may also be prescribed to dissolve blood clots that have formed near the brain. Treatment should be administered as soon as the TIA occurs in order to reduce the likelihood of a stroke. Though it may not prevent the stroke from developing all the way through, it could reduce the severity if one does occur.

A carotid endarterectomy may be performed to prevent fatty acids from developing in the carotid arteries. The procedure requires an incision, followed by the removal of plaque in the artery.

An angioplasty may also be recommended for some patients. The treatment opens the clogged artery and allows blood to flow through the region. A stent is required to help keep the artery open.

Stroke Scale

The National Institutes of Health Stroke Scale analysis assesses the severity of a stroke on a score of 0 to 3 based on eleven separate characteristics. The higher the score, the more severe a stroke.

The Stroke Scale analysis includes:

1. Level of consciousness
2. Horizontal eye movement
3. Visual acuity
4. Facial impact
5. Arm movement
6. Leg movement
7. Limb ataxia
8. Sensory support
9. Language impacts
10. Speech ability
11. Ability to identify various stimuli

All eleven signs should be carefully assessed.

Temporal Arteritis

Temporal arteritis is also known as giant cell arteritis. The intima, media and adventitia layers in arteries near the scalp become inflamed, thus resulting in substantial harm to the area.

Headaches can develop, with the pain spreading to the jaw, neck and other nearby areas. Vision changes may also develop in some patients. A patient's veins around the scalp may start to bulge, thus creating noticeable changes in the patient's appearance. Temporal arteritis may trigger blindness in some people. The condition could potentially become permanent depending on its severity.

A CRP test, which measures the C-reactive protein in the bloodstream, can help diagnose temporal arteritis. The protein is generated by the liver when there is inflammation in the body. An ultrasound may be performed on the scalp to assess blood flow.

Prednisone and other corticosteroids should be prescribed. The patient should be encouraged to start a healthy diet and exercise routine to reduce blood pressure and prevent the condition from flaring up any further in the future.

Failure to quickly and appropriately treat temporal arteritis could result in permanent blindness. Vision loss due to the condition takes about two weeks to become permanent.

Migraine Headache

A migraine headache is extremely intense and can result in a pulsing or throbbing sensation.

A migraine has four stages:

1. Prodrome

The prodrome stage causes increased thirst, mood changes and constipation to develop a few days before the migraine occurs.

2. Aura

The aura develops gradually as the migraine headache is about to start. The aura can last for about an hour. The patient may notice bright lights, numb sensations in the extremities and could have difficulty speaking or focusing on things.

3. Attack

A migraine attack involves intense pain and can last for up to 72 hours. The pain develops throughout the head and results in a throbbing or pulsing sensation. The patient may also become overly sensitive to light and touch.

4. Post-Drome

The post-drome part of the migraine involves a patient feeling very fatigued. The person may become sensitive to light. The post-drome stage lasts for about a day on average. Sudden head movements could result in a repeat of the attack stage.

A person may have migraines a few times in a month, or they can occur on rare occasions without warning.

A lab test may be performed to identify any inflammatory markers. An imaging test may also assess brain function.

Medications may be prescribed to those who experience regular migraines. Antiemetics may help reduce the intensity of vomiting or nausea.

An MRI may be used to rule out tumors or other growths in the brain that could be causing the migraines.

Increased Intracranial Pressure

An increased intracranial pressure (ICP) headache is triggered by a brain injury or another related condition. The headache may develop due to excess cerebrospinal fluid around the brain, swelling in the brain or bleeding in the brain.

An ICP headache involves a change in the volume of the compounds inside the cranium. Extracellular fluid should comprise 85 percent of the volume. Ten percent of the volume should be blood, while the remaining five percent is the cerebrospinal fluid necessary for protecting the brain. A change in the volume totals will result in an ICP headache.

A spinal tap may be used to measure the total pressure of the cerebrospinal fluid. An increase in pressure may indicate an ICP headache.

The headache will trigger many symptoms similar to a regular headache, including blurry vision, weakness in the body and a lack of energy. Neurological damage may develop if the headache is not appropriately treated.

The elevated cerebrospinal fluid or excess blood in the brain must be drained to resolve the situation. Medication may be provided to reduce the swelling, but this only works when all affected parts of the brain are treated simultaneously. Any infections or tumors must be treated or removed.

In particularly severe cases, a part of the skull may need to be removed to ease the swelling.

Meningitis

Meningitis is an inflammation of the brain and spinal column. An infection triggers the condition in the meninges or membranes near the brain and spinal column.

A viral infection can produce meningitis, although a bacterial or parasitic infection may occur in some cases. The condition causes flu-like symptoms, although vomiting and a stiff neck may occur in some cases. Headaches might also develop, potentially intensifying as the condition worsens.

Meningitis is fatal if not treated. A patient may develop brain damage, seizures or kidney failure.

Meningitis is not as common as it once was, as the MCV 4 meningococcal vaccine has helped to reduce the occurrence.

A lumbar puncture can help assess cerebrospinal fluid for signs of infection. The brain should be monitored during the puncture to ensure a hernia of the brain tissue does not develop due to the CSF being drained in the treatment process.

Intravenous antibiotics should be administered to treat the meningitis infection. The antibiotic administered will vary based on the bacterium causing the problem. A patient's sinuses may need to be drained. Bed rest is advisable. A patient should remain well hydrated.

Rehabilitation is often necessary for patients who have experienced meningitis. The duration may vary due to the potential damage to the nervous system. Individuals affected by bacteria-related meningitis will require the greatest amount of recovery time, especially if they have had significant breathing-related concerns.

Dementia

Dementia is a general term used to denote a period of cognitive decline. This is one of the more common neurological concerns that patients may experience.

Dementia may occur due to the ongoing destruction of neurological tissue. A person who has experienced a stroke may be at risk of experiencing dementia. Repeated head injuries may also be a contributing cause of dementia.

A patient may be diagnosed with dementia following a general examination. A CT scan or MRI can assess the brain's functionality and can be used to examine reactions to various stimuli.

Dementia is irreversible. A patient with dementia should be encouraged to undergo occupational therapy to help him or her cope. A person's living environment may also need to be modified to help the individual cope more easily with daily activities.

Alzheimer's Disease

Alzheimer's disease is a common form of dementia that causes the brain cells to progressively die off. Alzheimer's-afflicted individuals will repeat things and forget basic information. They may struggle with focus and ability to understand other's speech.

Alzheimer's is often a result of plaques or tangles caused by tau proteins in the brain. The brain cells will die off due to those cells not receiving the support they require for proper health. This causes the brain to shrink. Older people are more likely to experience Alzheimer's, although people of any age may experience it due to head trauma.

People who are suspected of having Alzheimer's should be tested for other conditions that could mimic the symptoms of the disease. A blood test may identify if the patient has a thyroid or vitamin-related deficiency. An MRI or CT scan may be used to locate any tumors that could be causing the problem. Essentially, such diagnostics are used to rule out what the condition is not, eliminating alternatives until the ultimate diagnosis remains Alzheimer's.

Alzheimer's does not have a cure, but medications such as memantine may help with slowing down the effects and progress of the disease.

A patient with Alzheimer's should be regularly monitored to ensure the person does not become lost, disoriented or otherwise put him or herself at risk of harm.

Myasthenia Gravis

Myasthenia gravis (MG) involves the cessation of clear communication between nerves and muscles in the body, thus causing weakness all over.

MG causes symptoms such as drooping eyelids or double vision. The face and throat muscles may become weak to the point where it's difficult for a person to speak, swallow or change facial expression. A patient who has difficulties with any of these activities should consult a doctor as soon as possible.

MG can occur in people of varying ages. However, it is more likely to occur in women under 40 and men over 60.

Antibodies may produce the effects associated with MG. The receptors for the neurotransmitter acetylcholine may break down and wear out. The muscles will not receive the nerve signals that they require, thus causing general weakness. The thymus gland may also develop tumors that can cause difficulties with hormone regulation, including those responsible for regulating the development of muscle control.

A neurological exam should be performed before diagnosing the person with the condition. The patient's reflexes, muscle strength, muscle tone and coordination should be assessed. A blood test can identify any unusual antibodies. An MRI may be performed on the thymus gland to identify tumors or any other growths in the area which could be contributing to the problem.

Medications that may help in reducing the severity of MG include immunosuppressant treatments, corticosteroids and cholinesterase inhibitors. A thymectomy may also be required, wherein the thymus gland is removed.

Both relapses and remissions can occur within this condition. Infections may trigger relapses.

Guillain-Barré Syndrome

Guillain-Barré syndrome (GBS) is a neurological disorder where the immune system attacks the body's nerves. Nerve cells are damaged to where the body can no longer manage its regular activities. This includes the body potentially developing paralysis in various parts.

A person's extremities will experience weakness and a tingling sensation at the start. A patient might experience stomach flu or a respiratory infection prior to the first signs of GBS. He or she may begin to struggle with regular physical activities, developing leg weakness and pain. It may become difficult for some patients to control their bowel or bladder functions.

A spinal tap procedure is recommended for assessing unusual changes in antibody behavior and counts may be noted. A nerve conduction study may be performed. This involves electrodes being taped to the skin near the nerves. A shock is administered to assess how fast nerve cells are moving.

Although GBS cannot be cured, it is possible for a person to recover from the symptoms. There is a potential for a relapse of those symptoms to occur, even if they are well controlled for a time. A plasma exchange may help with replacing the antibodies with healthier ones that will not attack the nervous system. Immunoglobulin therapy may also be administered. Medications to prevent blood clots may also be recommended for patients who are immobilized for prolonged periods due to GBS.

Multiple Sclerosis

Multiple sclerosis (MS) is a chronic condition that involves the destruction of the myelin sheath in the cells around the central nervous system. The destruction leads to the buildup of plaque in the central nervous system. Activated T cells will enter the system, crossing the blood-brain barrier. The immune system will start attacking the healthy system with the belief that it is a foreign body.

MS can occur on and off. There may be cases where a person goes into remission for months or years at a time before the MS returns.

The most common form of MS is a relapsing-remitting form. In this case, a person will experience flare-ups of MS over time. The flare-ups will become progressively more intense and noticeable. The symptoms that occur after flare-ups will not be as strong, but they will become more significant after each flare-up.

A primary progressive form of MS involves the condition worsening over time. A secondary progressive form will entail the condition being frequently active and will not entail any remission, but the condition will consistently relapse and remit after a while.

A patient will develop numbness in various parts of the body, often on one side at a time. Double vision and blurry vision can also occur.

Over time, MS may worsen to where a person experiences difficulties with mobility. The general progression of MS will vary by patient.

MS can occur at any age. People who have been exposed to the Epstein-Barr virus in the past are at a greater risk. MS is also more likely to occur among people who have family members who have developed the condition.

Diagnosing MS involves various tests to rule out other physical conditions. A spinal tap or lumbar puncture removes a small amount of fluid from the spinal canal in order to assess antibodies. A blood test may also be part of the diagnostic process.

An MRI can identify lesions or growths within the brain and spinal column.

Corticosteroids may be prescribed to reduce nerve inflammation. A plasma exchange may be necessary in cases where symptoms don't respond to steroid treatments. Other medications may reduce the instances of relapses.

Seizure-Related Concerns

A seizure involves unusual changes in the brain's electrical activity. Depending on the severity, the damage may be significant.

Types of Seizures

Seizures may occur in many forms:

1. Focal

A focal seizure is a partial seizure. It only occurs in one part of the brain. The seizure begins at a specific focal point. A patient may lose consciousness during the seizure.

2. Absence

An absence seizure is a generalized seizure, which means that activity occurs in both hemispheres in the brain. The action causes unconsciousness, but no convulsions. An absence seizure can last for about 15 seconds at a time. The patient will not have any memory of the seizure after it takes place. An absence seizure may also be referred to as a petit mal seizure.

3. Convulsive

A convulsive seizure causes electrical changes throughout the whole brain. A person will lose consciousness and experience stiffened muscles, elevated bladder pressure and sudden twitching. The seizure will last for a few minutes. Patients are not believed to suffer brain damage during a convulsive seizure.

4. Atonic

An atonic seizure can cause unconsciousness and will not result in any convulsions. The seizure lasts for a few seconds. The patient may fall on the floor due to the seizure.

5. Tonic

During a tonic seizure, a patient experiences facial spasms or muscle spasms elsewhere in the body. Depending on the severity, the seizure may cause a loss of bowel control.

6. Clonic

A clonic seizure involves the body losing control of its functions. The patient may start to experience various jerking motions triggered by the seizure.

Risk Factors

A patient may develop seizures based on various situations relating to cranial health. A patient with cerebral edema or head trauma will have a higher risk of developing seizures in many forms.

Patients with epilepsy can also develop seizures, particularly those not on antiepileptic medication.

Drug or alcohol withdrawal may cause concerns in some patients due to the nervous system being awakened from a depressed state.

Individual triggers will vary by person, but exposure to flashing lights, intense physical stress and hyperventilation are all factors that may cause seizures to develop.

Diagnosis and Treatment

Seizures may be diagnosed based on the various types of movement that do or not occur during a specific kind of episode (i.e., convulsing). An electroencephalography may help with identifying dramatic changes in the patient's brain waves, including changes that occur when a seizure takes place.

An MRI can also be performed to rule out tumors or the potential for tumors. A tumor might trigger seizures and, if present, may need to be surgically removed.

Seizures may be treated through antiepileptic drugs. The effectiveness of medications will vary from patient to patient. A patient should be advised to avoid specific situations that may trigger seizures.

Phenytoin and benzodiazepine should be administered in cases where antiepileptic drugs are not working. Anesthesia may be necessary in other cases where a patient's pain or seizure-related complications become severe.

Hydrocephalus

Hydrocephalus, also called water on the brain, occurs when excess cerebrospinal fluid develops in the ventricles in the brain. The condition increases pressure within the brain.

Any person can develop hydrocephalus but it's more common in infants and the elderly. In children, hydrocephalus may be noted through an increase in head size, a bulging appearance at the top of the head, vomiting or sleepiness. Older people who experience hydrocephalus will develop a headache, fatigue, a loss of bladder control or a regular urge to urinate. Memory loss and a lack of balance may also occur among older patients.

Hydrocephalus may develop due to an obstruction in the brain, preventing fluid from flowing as it normally would.

An ultrasound, MRI or CT scan may help to identify hydrocephalus. The ultrasound is the most effective diagnostic process, as it can assess hydrocephalus even during a prenatal analysis.

A shunt must be inserted into a patient's head to relieve the pressure. A shunt features a flexible tube with a valve that prevents fluid from moving in the wrong direction. Hydrocephalus is life-threatening and fast treatment is vital.

A patient with a shunt should be monitored for nausea, fever, headaches, vision difficulties or abdominal pain.

Spinal Cord Injury

A spinal cord injury is an irreversible form of damage to the neurological system. The spinal cord cannot be restored or regrown. Such an injury may occur due to a traumatic injury, compression in the spinal cord or from ischemia triggered by the spinal arteries.

Segments

The severity of the spinal cord injury will depend on the segment of the spine that is injured. The segments in the spinal cord correspond to the nerves. The nerves are arranged from top to bottom as follows:

1. Cervical – C1 to C8
2. Thoracic – T1 to T12
3. Lumbar – L1 to L5
4. Sacral – S1

Severity of Injury

The level of the injury will be reflective of the segments in the spinal column that are injured. The condition is referred to as paraplegia if the injury is at the T1 to T5 nerve. This means that only the lower extremities in the body are influenced. An injury at the C1 to C7 level is a tetraplegic injury, which impacts both the upper and lower extremities alongside the body's general respiratory function.

A spinal cord injury may be complete or incomplete. A complete injury entails the patient losing all of his or her sensory and motor function below the injury. An incomplete injury means that the patient has some control over motor functions below the injury and may still have feeling in the area. The severity of an incomplete injury may vary.

Tests to assess the extent of a spinal cord injury may include an assessment of a patient's movements, bowel or bladder control, ability to sense touch and any reflex actions. Any pain or struggles breathing should also be factored into the diagnosis.

Identifying the Injury

Three tests are used to identify a spinal cord injury:

1. X-ray

An X-ray can be used to examine the spinal column and assess the severity of an injury. Any fractures, degenerative changes, tumors or other threats to the spinal column's health should be carefully examined.

2. CT scan

A CT scan may be used to study the discs in between the spinal vertebrae. These discs may become damaged or impaired due to illness or injury.

3. MRI

An MRI can identify any herniated discs triggered by the spinal cord injury. Blood clots and any other growths can also be seen with an MRI.

A thorough neurological exam should be performed by a doctor, along with a muscle strength test to identify how well the patient responds to various forms of stimulation.

Managing the Patient

A nurse and other professionals must be cautious when working with a patient who might have a spinal cord injury. The patient should not be moved much, as the injury could be worsened. The head and neck should be immobilized to further secure the stability of the spinal column.

Any cases of numbness or paralysis are cause for concern. They may be a result of bleeding and swelling in the spinal column, thereby worsening the injury. A spinal cord injury may be noticed anywhere from 48 to 72 hours after the injury occurs.

Emergency treatment of a spinal cord treatment is critical for a patient's recovery. Most patients who experience spinal cord injuries will be able to return home and eventually regain some form of independence. In other cases, a patient may never recover.

Shock Syndromes

Shock syndrome may develop in a patient due to the spinal cord injury. The syndrome may occur in one of three forms:

1. Hemorrhagic

A hemorrhagic shock is acute in nature. It occurs under the T6 nerve and can entail hypotension.

2. Spinal

Spinal shock involves a patient losing sensory motor functions. This loss will vary based on the particular nerves damaged by the injury.

3. Neurogenic

A neurogenic shock involves bradycardia, hypotension and vasodilation. The nervous system will experience significant impacts that may negatively influence the body's functions and how well it may identify sensations. Neurogenic shock occurs over the T6 nerve in most situations. Prednisone may be required to reverse the effects of neurogenic shock.

General Forms of Care

The forms of care that a patient will require after a spinal cord injury occurs will vary based on the patient's condition and particular type of injury.

General immobilization may be encouraged in the treatment process. Immobilization prevents the patient from shifting his or her body, lessening the chances of further damage to the neck, spinal column or other parts of the body.

Surgery may be required to remove herniated disks, bone fragments or fractured vertebrae that are compressing the spinal column.

Hypothermia may be induced in some patients for 24 to 48 hours to stop the death of cells and support the regeneration of nerves.

General rehabilitation is a necessity for patients with spinal cord injuries. Rehabilitation, guided by a trained medical professional such as a physical therapist, focuses on strengthening any muscles that have weakened in order to restore general mobility.

Medications may be prescribed for a patient's comfort, such as to relieve pain. Some medications may help restore a person's bowel or bladder control.

It may take months or years for a patient to recover. Some patients might experience minor improvements, others major improvements, while others may never recover at all.

Chapter 15 – Blood Transfusions

When a patient has experienced a substantial amount of blood loss, he or she may require a blood transfusion. Sometimes blood must also be replaced, such as during a surgical procedure.

A blood transfusion may be necessary when a patient experiences an illness, infection or other significant injury resulting in a sizeable amount of blood loss. A patient who is undergoing treatment for cancer may need a transfusion, especially in cases where blood cells are being killed off due to chemotherapy.

The Process

The blood transfusion process is as follows:

1. A patient's blood is drawn and blood type is confirmed.
2. An intravenous line is placed in the patient.
3. The blood that is to be provided to the patient is identified and matched with the patient's blood type.
4. The new blood that the patient requires is transfused via IV into his or her body.
5. Afterwards, the IV line is removed, and an appropriate dressing is applied over the site.
6. The patient's reaction to the transfusion should be carefully monitored.

The time frame for the process will vary by patient. In most cases, the transfusion itself lasts from one to four hours. The patient will then have to be monitored in a hospital for three to six days. The timing varies based on the severity of a patient's medical condition and the amount of blood transfused.

Possible Effects

The patient should be monitored after the blood transfusion process to ensure he or she does not experience any dangerous side effects. Some side effects include chills, fainting, flushing in the skin or shortness of breath.

An allergic reaction may occur, including hives and itching. Antihistamines may be prescribed to the patient as needed to treat such occurrences.

Blood Analysis

Blood which is to be transfused into a patient must be carefully analyzed not only for blood type but for bacteria. Such bacteria may cause an infection or shock, and may even be deadly in some cases.

The blood must be tested for various illnesses and diseases. This is especially the case for HIV. Although patients with HIV or AIDS are legally prohibited from donating blood, there is a potential that someone who has not been diagnosed may donate blood. Therefore, all blood must be rigorously tested prior to transfusion.

Blood's iron content should also be tested. Excess iron may cause difficulties in the liver, triggering hemochromatosis.

Types of Blood

It is critical for a patient to receive the correct type of blood in the transfusion process.

Blood is identified based on the antigens or proteins that are on the surfaces of the red blood cells. For instance, a patient with type A blood has A-antigens.

The Rhesus factor (Rh) dictates the form of blood. This is in reference to another antigen on the red blood cell. The protein may be positive or negative. Therefore, a patient with B-antigens and negative Rhesus factor antigens will have B-negative blood.

The key is to ensure that the blood being transferred matches what the patient needs. A failure to transfuse the correct blood type will result in blood cells clumping together, blocking vessels and potentially causing death if corrective treatment is not administered immediately.

In general, there are eight types of blood that may be divided up in many forms:

1. A patient will have an A, B, O or AB antigen.
2. The Rhesus factor will be positive or negative, thus further segmenting the blood that may be noted.

The standards for blood donations are as follows, as a person with a certain blood type is allowed to donate blood to the following parties:

A+ = A+, AB+

A- = A+, A-, AB+, AB-

B+ = B+, AB+

B- = B+, B-, AB+, AB-

O+ = A+, B+, O+, AB+

O- = any type of blood

AB+ = AB+

AB- = AB+, AB-

A patient with O- blood is a universal donor, meaning he or she can donate blood to any person. Meanwhile, an AB+ patient is a universal recipient in that he or she can receive blood of any type.

The A, B and O-positive forms of blood are the most common. AB negative is the rarest form of blood.

All blood types are inherited from family members. Some forms of blood may be found more in certain countries over others. An example of this is China, where Rh- blood is extremely rare.

All blood transfusions must be carefully planned to avoid complications from the transfusion.

Chapter 16 – Bed Positions

Various bed positions may be used when helping a patient who is in a hospital. The appropriate bed position should be based upon a patient's health and comfort. Proper body positioning, especially in the case of a traumatic injury, can be critical to a patient's recovery and/or in order to prevent worsening of an existing condition.

The following are standard bed positions:

1. Trendelenburg

In the Trendelenburg position, the head of the bed is lowered while the foot of the bed is raised. The position works well for patients with hypotension. The position supports venous return and facilitates blood flow.

2. Reverse Trendelenburg

The reverse Trendelenburg position is the opposite of the standard Trendelenburg. With the reverse Trendelenburg, the head of the bed is elevated and the foot of the bed is lowered. The position is ideal for patients with GI concerns, as it lessens esophageal reflux.

3. Fowler's

In the Fowler's position, the head of the bed is elevated 45 degrees. The hips may be flexed if necessary. A patient's head and lower back should be carefully supported. A footboard may also be provided to prevent foot drop from developing. The Fowler's position helps with a patient's ventilation. It may be helpful to people with cardiovascular issues or those who are recovering from thoracic surgery.

4. Semi-Fowler's

In the Semi-Fowler's position, the head of the bed is elevated 30 degrees. Patients with cardiac or respiratory issues will benefit from the Semi-Fowler's position. Individuals with nasogastric tubes should also benefit from the position.

5. Lateral

The lateral position requires the patient to lie on one side. The top leg is in front, while the knee and hip are both flexed. The position reduces pressure on the sacrum and helps patients on extended bed rest or those who spend a good deal of time in the Fowler's position. Support should be provided for a patient's head and neck in order to allow the patient to stay in the lateral position.

6. Sim's

In the Sim's position, the patient is placed halfway between the prone and lateral positions. The upper arm is flexed, while the lower arm is behind the patient. The legs are flexed, with the upper leg flexed a little more than the lower one. A pillow is placed between the patient's legs. The position is especially useful for patients undergoing an enema.

7. Supine

In the supine position, the pillow is placed under the patient's head and shoulders. Pillows may also go on the patient's sides to provide additional comfort and support. The supine position is standard positioning for most patients and is often used after surgery.

8. Prone

In the prone position, the head is turned to the side, while the patient lays on his or her abdomen. The arms may be flexed on each side of the head if necessary. A pillow should be placed under the patient's head and may also be placed under the lower legs to keep them slightly elevated. The prone position is not recommended very often as it can overextend the lower back. It may also cause added pressure to the chest, thus making it harder for the patient to breathe.

The Most Common Mistakes People Make When Taking the CMSRN Exam

This chapter will focus on the mistakes that you might make while taking the CMSRN exam. It's normal to make mistakes, and therefore important to know how to avoid these as much as possible and remain calm while resolving any issues encountered while testing. The key is to have a plan for how you're going to successfully complete your exam. In this section, we'll walk you through preparing such a plan.

Second-Guessing

When you are taking the CMSRN exam, you may find yourself second-guessing your ability to answer questions. The best way to avoid that is to plan your studies based on the various parts of the exam. Prior to the exam, consider what might appear in the various sections. You can use your knowledge of those sections to determine what you already know well and what you need to study prior to the test. You'll also gain confidence as you realize that you already know more than you think you do.

Not Feeling Prepared

Many people who complete the CMSRN exam often feel nervous about their ability to complete the exam. Such people might not feel prepared. The good news is that the CMSRN exam can be easy to manage when you understand the testing process. You can use the practice exams in this guide to give you a good idea of what that process will entail.

It is understandable that people who haven't been in school for a while might feel nervous about taking a test. But the tips in this guide, combined with the practice tests and a careful reflection upon your strengths and weaknesses, can help you feel much more confident on test day.

Being Anxious

Some of the most common reasons why people feel anxious about the CMSRN exam include:

- Worrying about what is and is not on the test
- Thinking that the test might be difficult
- Concerns over what might happen if they do not succeed
- Uncertainty over the time frame for completing the test

All those concerns are addressed in this guide, starting with a clear explanation of what is on the test. Therefore, by carefully studying this book, you'll be ahead of the game. While there are certainly difficult parts, thorough preparation will make sure you can tackle anything on the exam.

You also now know that if you don't pass the test, you can take it again. Plus you have been given tools to help assess your areas of strengths and weaknesses so that you don't repeat the same mistakes on the retest.

Finally, you have a clear understanding by now of how long the test is. When taking the practice exams, use that knowledge to guide you, in order to simulate a real-world testing experience.

Leaving Answers Blank

There might be times when you skip an answer. This isn't a good idea because you'll be penalized for the skipped question. If you at least attempt the question, eliminating as many of the answer options as you can so you narrow the possibilities down to one or two, you'll stand a chance of getting it right. Bear in mind that you can always go back and change your answer later. Just don't leave anything blank, in case you run out of time. Your best guess is better than none at all.

Not Noting the Directions

The following words may appear in some of the CMSRN exam questions you're asked to answer:

- Define – explain or provide a definition
- Explain – provide a description of something
- Analyze – review the individual elements involved in a question
- Diagnose – note the condition that a patient might have
- Not – explain which of the choices in a question is not applicable or correct based on the situation at hand
- Compare – explain the differences and similarities
- Contrast – the differences are the key, not the similarities

It's important to carefully read each test question and note these words to make sure you're answering correctly. In other words, you don't want to miss a "not" applicable, for example, and instead choose an answer that *is* applicable. It's easy to miss those little details if you're rushing or nervous, so be aware and read questions thoroughly.

Ignoring the Time

You only have a limited amount of time for completing the CMSRN exam. As such, you should plan a schedule for the test and then stick to that time frame. The schedule should include looking at how you're going to go through each set of questions and how you're going to plan your answers. Allotting yourself a certain amount of time for each question is a good idea. That time should include both reading the question and answering it.

Remember that you can go back to certain questions during the test, so don't spend too long on any question.

You should plan on finishing the test as early as possible, without rushing. Finishing early will allow you to go back and check your work.

Overthinking

Don't overthink things. Because of the limited time, you can't take extensive time on one single question. That will only impact how long you can take on other questions, which could ultimately prove to require more time—time which you wasted on the previous question. Stick to your preplanned time frame and if you're stuck, take your best guess. Then move on. The first answer that comes to mind is often correct.

Being Careless

It doesn't take much for a test-taker to become careless. But being careless can end up costing you valuable points. This goes back to reading questions carefully, noticing the small details that could otherwise trip you up. Even though you have a time limit, that's not an excuse to rush through and make silly mistakes that could be avoided had you just taken a few more seconds to carefully read both the question and answer.

Not Taking Advantage of Resources

There are many resources available to help you prepare for the CMSRN test, including this guide. You should take advantage of these many resources. Don't just assume that you know it all already—that's as bad as thinking that you know nothing. Take advantage of study guides, preparatory courses, tutors, etc.

Not Completing a Memory Dump

When you sit down to take the test, make sure that as soon as it's allowed, you jot down all the formulas you think you'll need, any key terminology, diagnostic measurements, etc. The more you write down immediately, the less you'll have to struggle to recall when you're taking the test and stressed. Not taking this step is a serious error that can cost you time later. Just make sure you don't do the memory dump before the test proctor allows you to begin the exam. Nothing can be written prior to the test's start.

Not Getting to the Testing Facility Early

As nervous as you'll be on exam day, make sure you get there early. Remember our tip to figure out where the testing facility is the day before, so you don't get lost. Lay your clothes out the night before and give yourself plenty of time to get there. That way, you won't be in a panic because of traffic, etc., or any other situation that might make you late. Instead, you can arrive at the facility early and take a few minutes to relax before the test, mentally preparing yourself for what's to come.

Making Common Testing Mistakes

These are some common testing mistakes you should avoid:

1. Accidentally skipping questions because you're rushing. Don't do that! Don't leave any questions blank either deliberately or accidentally.

2. Misreading a question. Read slowly and carefully. If it's a step-by-step question, read it both forwards and backwards.

3. Randomly going back to change your answers later out of nervousness, rather than logic. Your first guess has a high probability of being right, so don't change an answer unless you have a good reason.

4. Spending too long on one question. As mentioned before, this then costs you time for other questions, some of which may turn out to be harder and require more time. Stick to your preplanned time frame.

5. Reading the wrong thing from your scratch work. You'll be doing calculations and such during the exam, likely relying on the aforementioned memory dump. Just make sure you keep that information organized so you don't pick the wrong formula to use, for example, and then get a test question wrong.

Worrying About the Cost

You might be concerned about how much it costs for you to take the exam. It is true that the CMSRN isn't cheap, especially if you have to retake it.

Yes, it does cost a few hundred dollars every time you complete the test, but that is to help with funding the development and administration process for the test. The fact is that once you're certified, your salary will increase, as will your career opportunities, so it's worth the money.

Payscale.com estimates that CMSRN's earn about $78,000 a year on average. This is in comparison with the $65,000 total that a registered nurse earns on average, or the $70,000 that a charge nurse receives every year. Think of the cost of taking the exam as a small pittance in comparison with the great financial benefits that come with completing the exam. Cost simply should not be one of the things that worries you when you take the test.

The next few sections of this guide are the practice tests we've mentioned before. They're laid out to resemble a real CMSRN as much as possible, to help you understand the structure and content of the exam.

Test 1 Questions

1. A patient has ascites. What is a sign of ascites?
    a. High epinephrine levels
    b. Low plasma albumin levels
    c. High plasma oncotic levels
    d. Low blood pressure

2. What makes CA-MRSA unique compared to other types of MRSA?
    a. It is acquired in a hospital
    b. It is transmitted through sex
    c. It is transmitted through blood transfusions
    d. All of the above

3. Foreign body aspiration entails an object in the:
    a. Larynx
    b. Trachea
    c. Both A and B
    d. Neither A nor B

4. Which of these is not an example of COPD?
    a. Emphysema
    b. Bronchitis
    c. Asthma
    d. All of the above are examples of COPD

5. A patient requires supplemental oxygen for a pulmonary treatment. Which of the following is correct about the oxygen that must be administered?
    a. The oxygen must be consistent
    b. The pressure should be high
    c. The pressure should be low
    d. The oxygen must be fully humidified

6. A person has been diagnosed with Crohn's. Which of the following is an incorrect statement about that person and the disease?
    a. Crohn's can potentially be cured
    b. The person could develop arthritis as a result of Crohn's
    c. Vitamin B12 is critical to the health of someone with Crohn's
    d. The person should consult the doctor about his or her abdominal pain

7. What is one true factor about peptic ulcer disease?
  a. Stomach pain starts 30 minutes after eating
  b. Malignant tumors may develop
  c. An endoscopy is needed
  d. NSAID use may be a concern

8. A patient has sickle cell disease. Which of the following is a correct statement based on his or her medical condition?
  a. The person has less free hemoglobin
  b. Nitric oxide totals will drop
  c. Arterial pressure may change
  d. Sildenafil may resolve blood-related concerns

9. A person who has hepatitis C and significant liver damage may require:
  a. Antiviral medication
  b. Bed rest
  c. A liver transplant
  d. A blood transfusion

10. Which of the following is true of a patient with a peptic ulcer?
  a. The patient will vomit blood
  b. The patient will constantly feel hungry
  c. The patient may breathe irregularly
  d. The patient may develop diarrhea

11. What is one sign of cholecystitis in a patient who has sickle cell disease?
  a. Abdominal tenderness
  b. General abdominal pain
  c. Left upper quadrant pain
  d. Rebound tenderness

12. How large does a foreign body have to be before it can produce a blockage in the small intestine?
  a. 1 cm
  b. 2 cm
  c. 3 cm
  d. 4 cm

13. Is it safe to allow gastroenteritis to resolve on its own?
 a. Yes, in all cases
 b. Depends on the situation
 c. When there is bacteria present
 d. No, it is not safe

14. What are the granulomas in Crohn's disease?
 a. Inflammatory cells
 b. Lesions
 c. Irritation along the ends of the intestine
 d. Cases in which the intestine is dying off

15. A person who has ulcerative colitis is experiencing diarrhea. What should a nurse closely examine when it comes to this person's condition?
 a. The frequency of bowel movements
 b. Pain involved
 c. Pus in the bowel movements
 d. The solid or loose nature of the bowel movements

16. Cholecystitis can be caused by:
 a. Cystic duct blockage
 b. Liver damage
 c. Hyperglycemia
 d. Hypertension

17. Which of the following is an appropriate treatment of gastritis?
 a. Antidiarrheal medication
 b. Antacids
 c. Antibiotics
 d. All of the above

18. What scan may help with identifying a case of appendicitis?
 a. An ultrasound
 b. A CT scan
 c. An MRI
 d. All of the above

19. Which form of hepatitis is transmitted by exposure to contaminated water or food?

a. A

b. B

c. C

d. D

20. What is necessary for hepatitis D to develop?

a. Hepatitis A must also be present

b. Hepatitis B must also be present

c. Oxygen is required in order for the virus to develop

d. All of these things help hepatitis D develop

21. What can be said about chlamydia?

a. It can be resolved with antibiotics

b. It requires a person to abstain from sex

c. It cannot be treated

d. The patient does not have to inform other sexual partners about his or her condition provided it is treated

22. The external ventricular drain implanted in a patient's brain is not having the desired results. What should be done in this case?

a. A proximal flush

b. A distal flush

c. Review ICP totals

d. Call another resident or PA for help

23. What is an ideal ICP rating?

a. 15

b. 25

c. 35

d. 40

24. You notice an ulcer on the left buttock of a patient at a nursing home. What should you avoid doing when trying to resolve the situation?

a. Using an air mattress
b. Restraining the patient
c. Turning the patient on occasion
d. Using dressings to control the ulcer

25. A patient consistently develops kidney stones. What advice should a patient be given to help resolve the problem?

a. Avoid alcohol consumption
b. Add lemons or limes to his or her dietary routine
c. Avoid red meat
d. All of the above

26. Which of the following is not a factor for the development of a decubitus ulcer?

a. Older and weakening skin
b. Diabetes
c. Bowel retention
d. Peripheral vascular disease

27. What is necessary for helping to promote natural skin healing?

a. Skin hydration
b. Allowing blood to flow to the skin
c. Massaging the skin on occasion
d. Using a topical medication

28. An EKG is necessary for assessing:

a. Heart function
b. Lung function
c. Bladder function
d. Nerve function

29. A patient has a nasogastric tube. What test should be performed after the tube is inserted?

a. An ultrasound
b. A chest X-ray
c. An abdominal X-ray
d. An EKG

30. What test should be performed on a patient experiencing intense fatigue and lethargy?

a. A CT scan
b. A Pan culture
c. An airway exam
d. A fluid test

31. A patient requires intracranial surgery. When should antibiotics be prescribed?

a. Before the surgery
b. During the surgery
c. After the patient is stable
d. Avoid adding antibiotics

32. A person is contacting a hospital for information on a patient who has been admitted to the hospital. The caller claims to be the patient's cousin. The person is not legally identified as a family member of the patient, who cannot communicate. How should the nurse respond to the person asking for information?

a. Briefly summarize the patient's condition
b. Decline to provide information
c. Provide contact information for the patient's family
d. Have the person physically come to the hospital for a discussion or consultation

33. A patient's spleen has been removed. What vaccine should be administered?

a. Recombivax
b. Attenuvax
c. Tetanus
d. Pneumonia

34. A patient has a puncture wound. What vaccine should be administered?

a. Tetanus
b. Herpes
c. Hepatitis
d. Pneumonia

35. Attenuvax is a vaccine that may help prevent:

a. Chicken pox
b. Measles
c. Hepatitis
d. HIV

36. A patient is having a hematoma removed. The patient should receive a Lantus dose the night before. What should happen next?

a. Provide the full dose
b. Provide only half the dose
c. Avoid giving the dose
d. Contact an attendant about the situation first

37. What is the most important part of Maslow's hierarchy?

a. Self-actualization
b. Food
c. Money
d. Sex

38. Maslow's hierarchy states that before a patient can heal, that person must have:

a. Security
b. Pleasure
c. Financial support
d. Accompaniment

39. A patient develops a fever about a week after a surgical procedure. All but which of the following conditions will trigger the fever?

a. A line infection
b. A urinary tract infection
c. Deep vein thrombosis
d. An infection in the wound

40. Is it appropriate to give information about a patient over the phone to anyone?

a. If an attorney gives permission
b. Absolutely never
c. At all times
d. It depends on the patient's medical condition

41. Is it appropriate to provide a person who is grieving after a family member's death with antidepressants?

a. Yes
b. No
c. Depends on the patient's response
d. Based on the patient's preference

42. Ketoacidosis is frequently triggered by:
  a. Dehydration
  b. Hyperglycemia
  c. Hypotension
  d. Hypoxia

43. What can result from diabetic ketoacidosis?
  a. A urinary tract infection
  b. Stale breath
  c. Sudden bouts of activity
  d. All of the above

44. Which of the following is true of sickle cell anemia?
  a. It is genetic
  b. It increases the patient's risk of a stroke
  c. It increases the risk of heart attack
  d. All of the above

45. What form of treatment can help resolve sickle cell anemia?
  a. A blood transfusion
  b. Hydrogen chloride
  c. Vasodilators
  d. All of the above

46. Patients who use clopidogrel may experience:
  a. Hypotension
  b. Bleeding
  c. Coughing
  d. Erectile dysfunction

47. Anti-platelet medications should be provided after:
  a. A stroke
  b. A heart attack
  c. Heart surgery
  d. All of the above

48. Metabolic ketoacidosis may be diagnosed when the blood pH level goes over:
  a. 5.5
  b. 6.85
  c. 7.45
  d. 9.25

49. What is the first stage in the Kübler-Ross theory?
   a. Depression
   b. Anger
   c. Denial
   d. Bargaining

50. A urinary tract infection may develop due to:
   a. A lack of sugar in the urine
   b. Frequent urination
   c. Excess sugar in the urine
   d. The infection can occur at anytime

51. What can a complete blood count test identify in sickle cell anemia?
   a. The condition itself
   b. Nothing
   c. Unusual changes in blood cells
   d. Fluctuating results

52. The Kübler-Ross theory states that a person who does not feel sick is experiencing which emotion?
   a. Bargaining
   b. Anger
   c. Acceptance
   d. Denial

53. What can be said about the Kübler-Ross theory?
   a. All people experience all stages of the theory
   b. The stages always go in order
   c. People can return to individual stages
   d. All of the above can be said about the theory

54. A patient is going to receive a colonoscopy in the near future. How should the patient's diet be adjusted as he or she prepares for the procedure?
   a. He or she should consume red meat
   b. He or she should stay hydrated
   c. He or she should consume only pureed foods
   d. He or she should avoid taking any medication before the colonoscopy

55. What part of the endocrine system tells the pituitary gland to start and stop producing hormones?

a. Parathyroid
b. Hypothalamus
c. Pancreas
d. Ovaries

56. The parathyroid regulates what in the body?

a. Calcium
b. Sodium
c. Electrolytes
d. A and B

57. A patient with a goiter will feel:

a. Consistent pain
b. Dizziness
c. Difficulty swallowing
d. A loose sensation

58. Which vein moves oxygenated blood from the lungs toward the left atrium of the heart?

a. Pulmonary vein
b. Systemic vein
c. Superficial vein
d. Deep vein

59. Which of the following is true when a vaccine is administered to a person with HIV or AIDS?

a. Twice the total is necessary
b. The vaccine must be administered in a specific part of the body
c. The patient may develop a seizure in some cases
d. The vaccine is always inactivated

60. What should happen when the Q wave appears on an ECG readout?

a. The readout will go up
b. The readout will go down
c. The depth will appear the same all around
d. A stable line will develop

61. When examining the SA node, what should a nurse look for when diagnosing sinus bradycardia?

a. A rapid beat rate
b. An irregular heartbeat
c. A slow beat rate
d. Cases in which the heart stops and starts at random

62. A patient has a blood pressure total of 160/105. What should be done for this patient?

a. Increase water consumption
b. Administer fludrocortisone
c. Administer calcium channel blockers
d. All of the above

63. Which of the following will not help prevent an asthma attack from occurring?

a. Avoiding pet dander
b. Avoiding fragrances
c. Smoking outside the house
d. Treating any respiratory infections as soon as possible

64. What may occur when a patient uses prednisone for too long?

a. Clotting
b. Hyperactivity
c. Slow heartbeat
d. Excess weight gain

65. Hypomagnesemia may occur among patients with:

a. Heart failure
b. Seizures
c. Migraine headaches
d. Crohn's disease

66. What may be noticed when observing a patient who uses Pyridium for the treatment of a urinary tract infection?

a. Discolored urine
b. A feeling of fullness
c. Excessive fatigue
d. Increased irritability

67. As soon as an HIV diagnosis is made, which vaccine should a patient receive?
   a. Influenza
   b. HPV
   c. Pneumonia
   d. PCV13

68. A patient with a magnesium deficiency may experience this condition alongside hypomagnesemia:
   a. Hypercalcemia
   b. Hypernatremia
   c. Hypophosphatemia
   d. Hypokalemia

69. What should be done when using antibiotics for the treatment of colitis?
   a. Identify diarrhea episodes
   b. Ask if the patient is experiencing pain
   c. Monitor the patient's temperature for signs of a fever
   d. All of the above

70. What should a patient avoid consuming in order to prevent listeriosis?
   a. Carbonated drinks
   b. Sugary products
   c. Processed meats
   d. Pasteurized milk

71. Which of the following is part of a standard treatment for scabies?
   a. Hand washing
   b. Condom
   c. Lamisil treatment
   d. Permethrin treatment

72. Which of these conditions is the least likely to trigger heart failure or cardiac arrest?
   a. Tamponade
   b. Toxin
   c. Trauma
   d. Trichomoniasis

73. A nurse discusses a patient's current medical concerns with her. At what point should the nurse ask the patient questions about her condition's severity?

a. During evaluation
b. During implementation
c. During planning
d. During diagnosis

74. What form of cancer is common in AIDS patients?

a. Lung
b. Liver
c. Brain
d. Skin

75. Which of the following is a treatment for cystic fibrosis?

a. Chemotherapy
b. Surgery
c. Body weight management
d. Symptomatic treatment

76. Is it possible for cystic fibrosis to be cured through a lung transplant?

a. Yes, provided both lungs are transplanted
b. Yes, but only one lung needs a transplant
c. No, a transplant will not cure cystic fibrosis
d. It depends on the patient's age

77. During the implementation part of standard nursing care, the following occurs:

a. The treatment plan is carried out
b. Medical tasks are delegated to other parties
c. The patient is informed about treatment options
d. All of the above

78. How many diagnoses can be made during the treatment process?

a. Only one
b. Two if necessary
c. Three if possible
d. As many as needed

79. What may occur during the sedative withdrawal process?
   a. Hyperactivity
   b. Depression
   c. Seizures
   d. All of the above

80. A patient who experiences a significant asthma attack will be likely to experience all but which of the following?
   a. Chest pains
   b. Shortness of breath
   c. Fever
   d. Tinnitus

81. What is noticeable in an absence seizure?
   a. It develops due to physical activity
   b. It may arise during a migraine headache
   c. It occurs in children more often
   d. All of the above are applicable

82. What is the most prominent feature of a petit mal seizure?
   a. Short duration
   b. Consciousness is retained
   c. Disorientation
   d. Lack of facial motion

83. What may develop due to deep vein thrombosis?
   a. A pulmonary embolus
   b. Cardiac flutter
   c. Seizures
   d. Arthritis

84. The most common way to control celiac disease is:
   a. Surgery
   b. Medication
   c. Dietary changes
   d. All of the above

85. Septic arthritis may be diagnosed using a/an:
   a. Echo test
   b. X-ray
   c. NSAID
   d. Blood test

86. A patient claims that he sat on a toilet seat previously used by an HIV patient. He says that he may have come into contact with the HIV patient's urine and is worried. What should the nurse tell him?
   a. HIV cannot be transmitted through a toilet seat
   b. HIV cannot last long outside the patient's body
   c. HIV is not in the patient's urine
   d. The nurse should tell the patient all of the above

87. How long can HIV last in a patient's body without treatment before it becomes AIDS?
   a. One year
   b. Three years
   c. Five years
   d. Ten years

88. A fusion inhibitor is an HIV medication that prevents the development of HIV by:
   a. Preventing HIV from entering healthy cells
   b. Blocking infected cells from moving
   c. Blocking proteins from developing
   d. Killing off infected proteins

89. Is there a potential for different forms of HIV medication to interact with one another?
   a. No interactions will occur between HIV medications
   b. A patient should use only one medication at a time
   c. It depends on the specific products
   d. It depends on how advanced the HIV is

90. What should a patient with fecal impaction not consume?
   a. Oatmeal
   b. Lentils
   c. Fish
   d. Berries

91. Standard treatment for hypernatremia is:

a. Diuretics
b. Charcoal
c. Fluid replacement
d. Sodium sulfonate

92. A patient who underwent an appendectomy has been experiencing vomiting and is having difficulty moving his bowels. This patient may have:

a. Toxic megacolon
b. Intussusception
c. Ileus
d. Colitis

93. A toxic megacolon develops due to the distention in the colon. This is caused by:

a. Colitis
b. Crohn's disease
c. C. difficile bacteria
d. All of the above

94. What should a patient with gout do to prevent gout flare-ups or attacks from occurring?

a. Regulate alcohol consumption
b. Increase seafood consumption
c. Increase sugar consumption
d. Increase calcium consumption

95. Is it safe for a patient with gout to consume caffeine?

a. Coffee may help reduce symptoms of gout
b. Carbonated drinks can reduce symptoms of gout
c. Caffeine should always be avoided as it can exacerbate symptoms of gout
d. It depends on the patient's specific condition

96. When should a patient stop using warfarin?

a. When the patient feels excessively hungry
b. When the patient's knees start aching
c. When the patient becomes hyperfocused on his environment
d. When the patient's gums start bleeding

97. What should a person not consume when on warfarin?

a. Dairy
b. Green leafy vegetables
c. Sugars
d. Gluten

98. Percocet works as a narcotic. What is its action?

a. Depressant
b. Stimulant
c. Blood thinner
d. Bowel stimulant

99. What is the most significant concern pertaining to narcotics?

a. They may cause heart damage
b. They can increase fatigue in the bowel
c. They may raise blood pressure
d. It is easy to become addicted to them

100. All of the following are appropriate treatments for anemia except:

a. Reducing alcohol consumption
b. Exercising consistently
c. Avoiding smoking
d. Staying in a cold environment

101. A child could be at risk of developing priapism due to:

a. Sickle cell disease
b. Hypotension
c. A particular injury
d. ADD medication use

102. When a patient on medication becomes lethargic, this may be problematic because:

a. That patient may struggle to take her medication
b. The lethargy may trigger breathing difficulties
c. The medication she is on may not be as efficient
d. A and B

103. What does aspirin do when administered for an acute myocardial infarction?

a. Aspirin promotes vasodilation
b. Aspirin prevents blood from clotting
c. Aspirin thins out the blood
d. Aspirin keeps the heart from working too hard

104. The main purpose of beta-blockers is:

a. To reduce the heart's overall workload
b. To prevent clotting
c. To boost the heart's function
d. A and B

105. What blood pressure total may be interpreted as pre-hypertension?

a. 125/85
b. 115/75
c. 145/90
d. 140/95

106. A person who smokes has a blood pressure total of 135/80. What is the best course of action for this individual?

a. He or she should be advised to stop using tobacco
b. He or she should be prescribed an inhaler
c. He or she should have a heart exam
d. He or she should be encouraged to stay hydrated

107. What test is appropriate for identifying a pneumothorax?

a. An electrocardiogram
b. An echocardiogram
c. An X-ray
d. A blood test

108. Furosemide is appropriate for:

a. Treating edema
b. Controlling swelling due to heart failure
c. Controlling swelling due to kidney disease
d. All of the above

109. What type of food should a person who uses furosemide consume more of?

a. Corn
b. Carrots
c. Bananas
d. Watermelon

110. A patient with a family history of diabetes has an HbA1c total of 6.2. What is an appropriate part of treatment for the patient?

a. Check the patient's blood sugar total in a week
b. Encourage the patient to follow a low-sugar diet
c. Prescribe the patient metformin
d. Prescribe the patient levothyroxine

111. An HbA1c total review entails a look at blood sugar levels over a period of how much time?

a. One week
b. One month
c. Three months
d. One year

112. At what age should a patient have his/her first colonoscopy?

a. 40
b. 50
c. 60
d. 70

113. Which of these tests is not necessary for a patient who may have a pulmonary embolism?

a. An echocardiogram
b. An X-ray
c. An arterial blood gas draw
d. A ventilation perfusion scan

114. What is a sign of a fat embolism?

a. Reduced serum lipase levels
b. Reduced erythrocyte sedimentation
c. Reduced platelet totals
d. Elevated calcium levels

115. Renal stones may form due to the regular consumption of:

a. Antacids
b. Recreational drugs
c. Potassium
d. Vitamin C

116. What can happen in a patient's bloodstream after an injury?

a. A reduced red blood cell total
b. An increased white blood cell total
c. Elevated platelets
d. No real change

117. What should be monitored when a patient with hypertension is treated with carvedilol?

a. The patient's pulse should be monitored each day
b. The patient's reflexes should be monitored
c. The patient's blood sugar levels should be monitored
d. The patient's blood calcium levels should be monitored

118. What can carvedilol cause?

a. Bradycardia
b. Hyperglycemia
c. Nerve bruising
d. Hypocalcemia

119. A patient develops a swollen calf a few days after surgery. What is an appropriate treatment or next step?

a. Consult another physician
b. Massage the calf
c. Send the patient to the emergency room
d. Complete exercises on the patient's legs

120. A large amount of fat around the ______________ may suggest metabolic syndrome.

a. Waist
b. Chest
c. Neck
d. Legs

121. What nerves are likely to be harmed when a person develops uncontrolled diabetes?

a. Nerves in the eyes
b. Nerves in the extremities
c. Nerves in the urinary tract
d. All of the above

122. How does hyperglycemia or hypoglycemia affect wound healing?

a. Wounds are slow to heal in all cases
b. Wounds may become hard after a while
c. A patient might not become injured as well
d. Only those with hyperglycemia may experience a concern

123. When the pancreas is healthy and produces insulin, how does this affect a diabetic's condition?

a. The insulin is excessive
b. The body will not accept the insulin
c. The body may not have enough insulin
d. Nothing noteworthy happens

124. A patient has an elevated risk of developing condyloma acuminate based on:

a. Family history
b. Abstinence
c. Drug use
d. Pregnancy

125. When a patient has a lack of human growth hormone, he or she may develop:

a. Dwarfism
b. Hypotension
c. Acromegaly
d. Hypoglycemia

126. What type of vaccination can prevent genital warts from developing?

a. Measles
b. HPV
c. Hepatitis
d. Influenza

127. What is a likely symptom of a urinary tract infection?

a. Discharge
b. Fever
c. Pain when urinating
d. Flank pain

128. Priapism may result from:

a. Cocaine use
b. Anemia
c. A groin injury
d. Bladder cancer

129. What treatment is best for a patient with a calcium-based renal stone?

a. Increased milk consumption
b. Better hydration overall
c. Avoiding foods with purine
d. Consuming antacids

130. A patient suffering from urinary retention may have the following form of incontinence:

a. Stress
b. Urge
c. Overflow
d. Functional

131. A woman who is experiencing an intense level of uterine bleeding should be assessed using a:

a. Pap smear
b. Uterine biopsy
c. Pregnancy test
d. Pelvic review

132. A patient with Alzheimer's will experience brain damage triggered by:

a. Strokes
b. Lewy bodies
c. Amyloid-b plaques
d. Prion infections

133. What is responsible for the formation of Parkinson's disease?
   a. A stroke
   b. A spinal cord injury
   c. A prion infection
   d. Lewy bodies

134. A patient has uncontrollable tingling and weakness in the hands and feet. What should the nurse ask the patient before beginning treatment?
   a. When did the patient first notice the condition?
   b. What activities cause the patient's pain to worsen?
   c. Has the patient experienced an infection recently?
   d. Has the patient noticed symptoms like these in the past?

135. What complication relating to temporal arteritis should be treated first?
   a. Irritation in the lower extremities
   b. Vertebral fracture
   c. Blindness
   d. Infection

136. A patient is experiencing a fever and neck stiffness. What is one possible condition that these could be symptoms of?
   a. Meningitis
   b. Seizures
   c. Chronic back pain
   d. Spinal infection

137. What should be administered to a patient who has undergone an ischemic stroke?
   a. Alteplase
   b. Tenecteplase
   c. Streptokinase
   d. Urokinase

138. Which of the following is true about Alzheimer's medications?
   a. They can cure the condition
   b. They can produce remission
   c. They can slow the disease's progression
   d. They are most effective if administered early

139. A focal seizure is a seizure that:

a. Occurs in one hemisphere of the brain
b. Occurs throughout the entire brain
c. May appear without warning
d. May result in possible damage

140. Who is more likely to experience an absence seizure?

a. Children
b. Seniors
c. Those who have never experienced seizures before
d. Anyone can develop an absence seizure

141. What is the first step of treatment when resolving an airway obstruction?

a. A CT scan
b. A tracheostomy
c. Anti-inflammatory treatment
d. The Heimlich maneuver

142. A form of pneumothorax that occurs in a patient who has never experienced the condition before is known as:

a. Traumatic pneumothorax
b. Tension pneumothorax
c. Spontaneous pneumothorax
d. Any of the above

143. Anaphylaxis is an airway obstruction issue triggered by:

a. Choking
b. Humidity
c. Dry air
d. An allergic reaction

144. Standard treatment for anaphylaxis includes:

a. Supplemental oxygen
b. Beta-blockers
c. Vasodilators
d. Anti-inflammatory medication

145. What is not a part of Virchow's triad for diagnosing thrombosis?

a. Stasis of blood

b. Endothelial functionality

c. Blood coagulation

d. Blood pressure

146. A pulmonary embolism is tested through a D-dimer blood test. Which of the following indicates the presence of a PE?

a. High D-dimer results

b. Low D-dimer results

c. Dramatic changes in the D-dimer totals over time

d. D-dimer values make no difference

147. This blood sugar total (in mg/dL) is considered normal:

a. 60

b. 100

c. 150

d. 200

148. What form of sugar is necessary for facilitating natural physical functions in the body?

a. Fructose

b. Glucose

c. Sucrose

d. All of the above

149. A pregnant woman who develops gestational diabetes should be advised that:

a. The condition is lifelong

b. The condition requires an early delivery

c. The issue is temporary

d. The condition may be due to being underweight

150. A patient claims to be urinating far too often. What is one sign that this could be a symptom of developing diabetes?

a. Blood pressure changes

b. Hyperactivity

c. Lethargy

d. Weight loss

Test 1 Answers

1. **b.** A person with ascites will have low plasma albumin levels. The lack of pressure from plasma proteins will allow fluid to enter the wrong areas. Cirrhosis may develop in some cases.

2. **a.** CA-MRSA is a community-acquired condition contracted in hospital stays.

3. **c.** Foreign body aspiration involves an object in the larynx or trachea blocking the airway.

4. **c.** Asthma is not an example of COPD. COPD involves airflow being blocked in the lungs. Asthma may develop due to COPD, but it is not necessarily a form of the condition.

5. **d.** The supplemental oxygen must be fully humidified to allow it to easily circulate through a patient's body.

6. **a.** It is wrong to say that the disease can potentially be cured. Although a surgical procedure can remove parts of the intestine that have been damaged, the procedure will not cure the condition. The other three answers are accurate aspects of Crohn's.

7. **c.** An endoscopy is necessary to diagnose peptic ulcer disease. It will take a few hours for stomach pain to develop.

8. **b.** Nitric oxide totals will drop in the patient's body due to sickle cell disease. Hemolysis will develop and free hemoglobin will increase due to the unusual shapes of the blood cells.

9. **c.** A liver transplant is necessary in patients with hepatitis C who have significant liver damage. The liver will be unable to function correctly due to the damage.

10. **a.** The person may vomit blood due to a peptic ulcer. Not all vomiting episodes produce blood, though. B and C are incorrect, as the patient will feel full and bloated, plus some noticeable breathing difficulties will occur.

11. **b.** General abdominal pain will occur when a person experiences cholecystitis. The pain will spread and will not be limited to one particular quadrant.

12. **b.** A foreign body of 2 cm in size can get stuck in the GI system. A surgical procedure is necessary to remove any foreign body of that size or larger.

13. **b.** The answer depends on the situation. Any case in which there is no visible bacterium merits a wait-and-see approach.

14. **a.** Granulomas are inflammatory cells that form in the intestine. These cells can cause irritation and possible damage in the area.

15. **c.** There may be pus in the bowel movements of a person with ulcerative colitis. Blood may also appear in some cases, which is a sign of the severity of the condition.

16. **a.** A cystic duct blockage will cause cholecystitis to develop. The gallbladder will not receive the necessary bile flow that it requires to stay healthy.

17. **d.** All of the above—anti-diarrheal medications, antacids and antibiotics—can work. Antacids may work at the start, although whether or not they will be effective will vary based on a patient's individual condition.

18. **a.** An ultrasound is ideal for identifying appendicitis. The scan is especially useful for women, as the signs of appendicitis often match up with the signs of an undetected pregnancy.

19. **a.** Hepatitis A is transmitted by the consumption of water or food contaminated by the virus. Hepatitis B and C are transmitted by infected people, while hepatitis D requires hepatitis B in order to exist.

20. **b.** Hepatitis B must be present for hepatitis D to survive. The hepatitis B virus can produce hepatitis D after a while.

21. **a.** Chlamydia can be cured with antibiotics. The condition must be treated to ensure the patient does not develop inflammation or additional complications.

22. **d.** The nurse must call another resident or PA for help at this juncture, as there is the potential for the drain to have a clot. The nurse should not try to flush out the drain without assistance.

23. **a.** An ICP of 15 is ideal. The intracranial pressure total should be under 20. Any case in which the ICP is over 30 could result in a permanent brain injury.

24. **b.** You should not use restraints when taking care of a patient with an ulcer. Restraints keep a patient in the same position, thus making the ulcer worse.

Anything that reduces pressure on the body or promotes healing (like a dressing) helps.

25. **d.** All of the above solutions work. Kidney stones can be controlled by drinking more water and less alcohol. Red meat should be avoided in favor of low-calcium foods. Lemons and limes are particularly useful in that they can dissolve the stones.

26. **c.** Bowel movement retention is not a factor in the development of a decubitus ulcer. Rather, incontinence can be more of a threat. There is a concern of weakened skin developing an infection or diabetes triggering nerve damage in the area.

27. **b.** Allow blood to flow to the skin. Blood flow is critical for keeping skin nourished and healthy. D is incorrect in that not all topical medications will help heal skin.

28. **a.** An EKG will identify heart function. The electrocardiogram will identify signals coming from the heart and allow a medical professional to assess heart function.

29. **b.** A chest X-ray should be performed after the nasogastric tube is inserted. The X-ray can assess lung function and identify any other concerns.

30. **a.** A CT scan will identify why the patient is experiencing lethargy and fatigue. The scan can identify cerebral changes.

31. **c.** Prescribe antibiotics after the patient is stable. Antibiotics may not be necessary in every case.

32. **b.** Decline to provide information to the person asking for it. The information on a patient's health should be provided to only family members that the patient has designated as being allowed to receive that information or to someone who has power of attorney. This rule is in accordance with the Health Insurance Portability and Accountability Act.

33. **d.** A pneumonia vaccine should be administered after the patient's spleen is removed. The vaccine prevents pneumococcal sepsis from developing after the surgery.

34. **a.** The tetanus vaccine should be administered after a puncture wound in order to prevent a clostridium tetani infection from developing.

35. **b.** Attenuvax is a live rubeola vaccine that administers a small amount of the virus into a patient's body, thus preventing the measles from developing.

36. **d.** Contact an attendant about the situation first. The attendant should assess the patient's blood sugar levels. Lantus might interact with the body differently depending on when the vaccine is administered.

37. **b.** Food is the most important of the four parts listed in the question. Maslow's hierarchy of needs states that the patient must have food, water and sleep to thrive.

38. **a.** Security is high on Maslow's hierarchy. Feeling safe is critical to a patient's health.

39. **a.** A line infection will not trigger a fever after a surgical procedure. A urinary tract infection, wound infection, deep vein thrombosis or drug fever are more important concerns to watch for.

40. **a.** A nurse can provide information over the phone if an attorney gives permission based upon the power of attorney granted to certain individuals by the patient.

41. **b.** No, the person who is grieving after a family member's death should not be prescribed antidepressants. The person should be referred for grief counseling.

42. **b.** Hyperglycemia can trigger ketoacidosis, which can lead to dehydration and other conditions. Intravenous fluid hydration is recommended for the treatment of the condition.

43. **a.** A urinary tract infection may develop due to diabetic ketoacidosis. B and C are incorrect, as ketoacidosis produces a fruity-scented breath and lethargy.

44. **d.** All of the above can be signs of sickle cell anemia. It is a genetic condition that can increase the patient's risk of developing various complications.

45. **a.** A blood transfusion is necessary to replace the old cells that are malfunctioning with new ones.

46. **b.** Bleeding is an effect of clopidogrel. The medication focuses on preventing the development of platelets, thus preventing clotting. The patient should be monitored to ensure that bleeding does not occur and that any bleeding that does happen is controlled.

47. **d.** All of the above situations require antiplatelet medications.

48. **c.** A blood pH level of 7.45 or higher will trigger metabolic ketoacidosis.

49. **c.** Denial is the first stage, followed by anger, bargaining, depression and acceptance.

50. **c.** Excess sugar in the urine can cause a urinary tract infection. It may also lead to diabetic ketoacidosis.

51. **c.** Unusual changes in blood cells may be identified in the CBC test. This includes changes in the red blood cell count. But the CBC test is not as effective as a peripheral blood smear.

52. **d.** The patient is in denial at this point. Denial is a part of the Kübler-Ross theory that states that a person initially is not willing to believe that he or she is ill.

53. **c.** People can return to individual stages of the theory. A patient can potentially go from one stage back to another, especially in cases in which sudden changes in his or her condition occur.

54. **b.** The patient must stay hydrated for the colonoscopy. Water is recommended, although electrolytes are acceptable if they do not contain lots of sugars. Medication should not be discontinued unless a doctor says it is fine to do so.

55. **b.** The hypothalamus signals the pituitary gland to start and stop producing hormones. The hypothalamus connects directly to the nervous system.

56. **a.** The parathyroid regulates calcium levels in the body and in the blood. The parathyroid also regulates phosphorous levels.

57. **c.** A goiter will cause difficulty swallowing and breathing. A patient may not experience great pain, but may feel a tight sensation.

58. **a.** The pulmonary vein moves oxygenated blood from the lungs to the left atrium. The systemic vein moves the non-oxygenated blood to the right atrium.

59. **d.** The vaccine must be inactivated. Some vaccines are activated, which means they have a form of the illness that the person is being vaccinated against. An activated vaccine will trigger the condition in a patient with HIV or AIDS.

60. **b.** The readout goes down when the Q wave appears. The Q wave is followed by the R wave, the highest point in the ECG readout. The S wave then appears and should be as deep as the Q wave.

61. **c.** A slow beat rate is evident in cases of sinus bradycardia. A beat rate under 60 beats per minute can be diagnosed as sinus bradycardia.

62. **c.** The nurse must administer calcium channel blockers if the blood pressure is this high. The patient is experiencing hypertension at this point. A and B are incorrect, as they are treatments for when a patient has hypotension.

63. **c.** The asthma patient should not smoke outside the house, or anywhere for that matter. Smoking can trigger an asthma attack. This includes exposure to secondhand smoke.

64. **d.** Excess weight gain is a common sign of using prednisone for too long. Other effects surrounding prednisone use include acne, slow wound healing, sleep issues, nausea, an increased likelihood of developing infections and blurry vision.

65. **d.** Crohn's disease is a condition that can result in hypomagnesemia. This is an electrolyte imbalance that will impact the digestive system and result in illness. A patient requires a certain amount of magnesium each day to prevent the issue.

66. **a.** Discolored urine is an effect of Pyridium use. The urine may develop an orange-like tone. Other symptoms include itchiness, stomach pains and dizziness or nausea.

67. **d.** The PVC13 vaccine should be administered as soon as the patient is diagnosed with HIV. The other three vaccines are critical for all HIV patients, but the PVC13 vaccine reduces the risk of infections that might compromise the body.

68. **c.** Hypophosphatemia develops due to a lack of magnesium in the body. The condition occurs as the body consumes more phosphate due to there not being enough magnesium to utilize.

69. **d.** All of the above considerations are critical when colitis is being treated with antibiotics. Antibiotics should prevent diarrhea from occurring and should resolve pain and fever-related concerns. There may be cases in which antibiotics are not working as well as hoped. In such cases, a surgical procedure may be required to resolve the issue.

70. **c.** Processed meats should be avoided when aiming to prevent listeriosis. Listeriosis can spread from contaminated food. Processed meats such as hot dogs and various lunch meats may become contaminated after being cooked and before they are packaged.

71. **d.** A permethrin treatment will help treat scabies. A topical treatment allows the condition to be treated directly.

72. **d.** Trichomoniasis is unlikely to trigger a cardiac episode. Trichomoniasis is a sexually transmitted disease that does not influence the heart's functionality. The other three answers are all things that can cause cardiac arrest.

73. **c.** The planning stage should occur at this point. Planning entails looking at what can be done to resolve the patient's medical issues.

74. **d.** Skin cancer is often seen in patients with AIDS. Kaposi's sarcoma is a common symptom of AIDS.

75. **d.** Symptomatic treatment is the only solution for cystic fibrosis. The condition does not have any cure.

76. **c.** The transplant will not work. Although the patient might have healthier lungs at the start, those new lungs will eventually be affected by CF. Thus, the transplant will not provide any long-term relief.

77. **d.** All of the above considerations are to be noted. The treatment must be carried out, and all parties involved should recognize their roles. But the patient also has to be informed about the treatments involved so that they feel comfortable.

78. **d.** The nurse can make as many diagnoses as needed. Additional testing may be required depending on the severity of the condition.

79. **c.** Seizures can occur as the patient stops experiencing the calming sensations produced by a sedative, thereby overwhelming the nervous system.

80. **d.** Tinnitus is not a condition that can develop due to an asthma attack. While the chest may experience pain, it will not trigger hearing-related issues.

81. **c.** An absence seizure occurs in children more often than adults. The unusual electric activity in the still-developing brain will cause a seizure that lasts for a few seconds at a time.

82. **a.** A petit mal seizure lasts only a short time. The condition can last for about 15 to 30 seconds at a time. Various facial movements, most of which are uncontrolled, will also develop during the seizure.

83. **a.** A pulmonary embolus may occur due to DVT. The clot may move to the lungs. This does not occur every time, but it is a threat.

84. **c.** Dietary changes are the only necessary treatment for celiac disease. The condition is triggered by the consumption of gluten. Therefore, avoiding gluten consumption will resolve the problem.

85. **d.** A blood test helps with identifying septic arthritis. The condition develops when a blood infection attacks the joints.

86. **d.** The nurse should tell the patient all those things in order to assuage the fear of contracting the disease. The patient should be advised that HIV does not appear in a patient's urine, so it would not be on a toilet seat. And even if it was somehow, the virus would die off shortly outside the body.

87. **d.** HIV can last for ten years without treatment before it becomes AIDS. The specific time frame will vary based on the condition.

88. **a.** A fusion inhibitor will prevent HIV from entering healthy cells. A CCR5 antagonist can do the same.

89. **c.** The potential for an interaction to occur depends on the specific medications. The proper drug cocktail for the treatment of HIV will be determined based on the patient's individual needs and on how medications interact with each other.

90. **c.** A patient with a fecal impaction should not eat fish as fish does not have enough fiber, unlike the other options.

91. **c.** Fluid replacement is recommended in the treatment of hypernatremia.

92. **c.** An ileus may develop when the patient is vomiting and not fully emptying his or her bowels. An ileus develops due to a GI tract malfunction.

93. **d.** All of the above concerns are problems that can cause a toxic megacolon to develop. The distention in the colon occurs due to Crohn's or the C. difficile bacteria. Ulcerative colitis is a significant concern as well.

94. **d.** The patient should increase his or her calcium consumption in order to prevent gout flare-ups from occurring. Seafood, sugar and alcohol should not be consumed by a patient with gout as they can worsen the condition.

95. **a.** Coffee contains enough caffeine to help ease the symptoms of gout. However, coffee should be consumed only without added sugars. Sugar can trigger gout-related symptoms. Therefore, caffeinated carbonated drinks that are filled with sugar should be avoided.

96. **d.** Warfarin should not be used when a patient's gums are bleeding. Warfarin is designed to help treat blood clots and prevent them from occurring.

97. **b.** Green leafy vegetables should not be consumed while using warfarin. Vegetables like spinach or kale contain high amounts of vitamin K and may reverse the positive effects of warfarin.

98. **a.** Percocet, also known as oxycodone, works as a depressant. The medication treats intense pain.

99. **d.** It is easy to become addicted to narcotics. These medications produce intense sensations in the nervous system that can relax the body. Sometimes the medication may cause a condition to become more intense when it returns, although the effectiveness of the medication may vary based on the treatment.

100. **d.** A patient with anemia should not be in a cold environment. A sickle cell crisis may develop due to cold temperatures.

101. **a.** Sickle cell disease will cause a child to develop priapism. Although the condition is more prominent among adults, a child could develop the issue due to the blood cells sticking in varying parts of the body. The cells may stay in the penile area, thus triggering priapism.

102. **d.** A and B are appropriate answers. Lethargy may make it harder for a person to breathe when taking the medication. The patient may also have a hard time orally ingesting the medication.

103. **b.** Aspirin is an antiplatelet agent, which means that it prevents platelets from sticking together and, therefore, prevents clotting.

104. **a.** Beta-blockers reduce the heart's overall workload. The medications help with resolving blood pressure issues through vasodilation.

105. **a.** 125/85 is a case of pre-hypertension. The systolic pressure goes from 120 to 139, while the diastolic goes from 80 to 90. Either of these is a sign of pre-hypertension. B is an example of hypotension, while C and D are both cases of hypertension.

106. **a.** The nurse should ask the patient to stop using tobacco and to monitor his or her blood pressure.

107. **c.** An X-ray may help identify a pneumothorax. An ECF may identify problems with blood flow but may not necessarily pick up on the exact problem.

108. **d.** Furosemide or Lasix is appropriate for all of the above. The medication is a diuretic that treats edema or fluid retention and swelling due to issues in the liver, kidneys, heart and other organs.

109. **c.** Bananas should be consumed while using furosemide. A patient may develop hypokalemia due to furosemide or Lasix being a strong diuretic. Bananas contain potassium, which offsets the threat of hypokalemia.

110. **b.** The nurse should encourage the person to maintain a low-sugar diet. A patient with a blood sugar total of this level has an elevated risk of developing diabetes. This is especially true if that person has a family history of the condition.

111. **c.** The measure works for three months. The HbA1c total is a measure of blood sugar based on an average within a certain period of time.

112. **b.** A person needs his or her first colonoscopy at 50 years of age. This is around the time when the patient may experience colon issues for the first time. A colonoscopy may be performed sooner, although that is mainly for people with a family history of certain colon-related issues.

113. **a.** An echocardiogram is not necessary for a PE diagnosis. The echocardiogram will assess the heart. The other treatments are suitable.

114. **c.** Reduced platelet totals will develop when a fat embolism occurs. Fatty acids will stay in one place, thus making it harder for platelets to form.

115. **a.** Antacids can cause renal stones to develop. Antacids often contain calcium and magnesium, which can trigger the production of such stones.

116. **a.** A reduced red blood cell total will develop. It is unclear why patients experience this drop.

117. **c.** A patient's blood sugar levels should be assessed when treating hypertension with carvedilol. The medication may cause hypoglycemia, which can be especially dangerous in diabetic patients.

118. **a.** Bradycardia may develop when a person is taking carvedilol. The condition causes the heart rate to drop.

119. **a.** It is best to consult another physician for help. Massaging the calf or having the patient do exercise would be inappropriate, as doing so could cause the clot to move to another part of the body.

120. **a.** The waist can develop excess body fat due to metabolic syndrome.

121. **d.** All of the above areas can be harmed due to diabetes. Nerves may be damaged and tear apart depending on the condition.

122. **a.** Wounds are slow to heal in all cases. Dramatic shifts in blood sugar can weaken the body's recovery process regardless of whether the patient has hyperglycemia or hypoglycemia.

123. **b.** The body will not accept the insulin. The body's cells will not absorb it regardless of how much insulin is produced.

124. **c.** Drug use can cause condyloma acuminate to develop in the body. The condition is also known as genital warts. Drug use includes the improper use of birth control drugs. The sexual activities that one engages in might become a concern.

125. **a.** Dwarfism occurs when a person does not have enough human growth hormone.

126. **b.** The human papilloma virus vaccine (HPV) helps to neutralize the bacteria that cause genital warts.

127. **c.** Pain when urinating may be a sign of a UTI. The lymph nodes may also become enlarged.

128. **c.** A groin injury can increase the risk of priapism. This may be due to the blood not flowing properly in the injured area.

129. **b.** The patient should drink more fluids. Adding calcium to the diet through milk consumption will only worsen the problem.

130. **c.** Overflow incontinence occurs due to urine retention. The bladder is filled with more urine than expected, thus causing part of it to be involuntarily released.

131. **c.** A pregnancy test should be performed. Uterine bleeding is often a sign that a woman is pregnant.

132. **c.** Amyloid-b plaques can destroy brain tissue in a patient with Alzheimer's. The plaque will form in the cerebral cortex.

133. **d.** Lewy bodies will result in the development of Parkinson's. Such bodies harm the nervous system.

134. **c.** The person should be asked whether he or she has experienced an infection recently. The condition may have an impact on the patient's breathing if not swiftly treated.

135. **c.** Blindness is a part of temporal arteritis that should be treated first. The blindness triggered by the condition may be irreversible, thus requiring treatment as soon as possible.

136. **a.** Meningitis can occur in this situation. A stiff neck may be a sign of an infection that is starting to spread within the body. Further monitoring may be necessary.

137. **a.** Alteplase is appropriate for the treatment of an ischemic stroke. The treatment will not produce as many adverse results.

138. **c.** Medications for Alzheimer's can slow the progression of the disease. Alzheimer's does not have a cure, nor can it go into remission.

139. **a.** A focal seizure occurs in one hemisphere of the brain. A generalized seizure occurs in both hemispheres.

140. **a.** Children are more likely to experience absence seizures. Such seizures will not last as long as others and a patient is unlikely to remember them afterwards.

141. **d.** The Heimlich maneuver should be performed first. The treatment may help with dislodging items that are immediately noticeable. A tracheostomy should not be performed unless the Heimlich maneuver is not working.

142. **c.** A spontaneous pneumothorax occurs in patients who have never experienced the condition before.

143. **d.** Anaphylaxis is an airway obstruction triggered by an allergic reaction. The allergen, whether it entails a food product or chemical, will trigger intense inflammation in the airways. The airways may tighten and cause extreme breathing issues.

144. **d.** Anti-inflammatory medication should be provided to a patient experiencing anaphylaxis. Antihistamines may also be prescribed to ease the pain after the inflammation lessens.

145. **d.** The blood pressure total is not a part of Virchow's triad. The triad entails excess coagulation, endothelial malfunctions and blood stasis.

146. **a.** High D-dimer results are signs of PE. The total states that there are excess protein fibers in the blood.

147. **b.** 100 mg/dL is a normal blood sugar level. A is a case of hypoglycemia, C entails above-average blood sugar and D involves hyperglycemia.

148. **b.** Glucose is necessary for regular body functions. Glucose levels that are out of control may indicate diabetes.

149. **c.** The issue of gestational diabetes is temporary. The condition resolves itself after the mother gives birth. Gestational diabetes may not produce many symptoms.

150. **d.** Weight loss may be noted when a person urinates too often. A sudden amount of weight loss due to excess urination may be a sign of developing diabetes.

Test 2 Questions

1. Chvostek's sign can be noted in the face. Signs of the condition include:
   a. Paralysis
   b. Blushing
   c. Twitching
   d. Shaking

2. Hypemic hypoxia occurs when:
   a. The blood cannot carry oxygen
   b. The patient cannot find oxygen
   c. Blood flow is inhibited
   d. Blood flow is too strong

3. Hemochromatosis can be diagnosed by looking at iron stores in the:
   a. Joints
   b. Pancreas
   c. Liver
   d. All of the above

4. Which organ is usually the first to be negatively impacted by blood-related conditions?
   a. Heart
   b. Liver
   c. Kidney
   d. Bladder

5. A patient has experienced an injury and is being observed. The patient has a high blood alcohol content and is slurring his or her words. The person has a history of alcohol abuse. The CT scan of the head was negative. What is the patient's likely condition?
   a. Alcohol withdrawal
   b. Depression
   c. Alcohol intoxication
   d. Delusional disorder

6. Which of the following is likely the above-mentioned patient's blood alcohol content?

a. 4
b. 6
c. 8
d. Any of those

7. What does a bolus do?

a. Provides immediate relief
b. Helps to remove a compound
c. Treats a patient's seizures
d. Works to administer a drug in a specific time frame

8. Lanoxin is necessary for the treatment of:

a. Atrial fibrillation
b. Seizures
c. High blood pressure
d. Hypotension

9. What happens when the transport of sodium is interfered with?

a. Effects of Parkinson's may be minimal
b. Blood sugar levels will decline
c. Blood pressure levels will decline
d. Cerebrospinal fluid production is lessened

10. When taking care of a patient who is not responding, what should be done last?

a. Assessing the airways
b. Checking the patient's breathing
c. Monitoring the patient's consciousness
d. There is no distinct order of treatment that should be followed

11. A patient has been prescribed Pyridium. What side effects are possible?

a. Jaundice
b. Bleeding
c. Hyperactivity
d. Excess awareness

12. Who is more likely to experience the effects of hypoxia?
    a. A long-distance runner
    b. A fisherman
    c. A mountain climber
    d. A police officer

13. Histotoxic hypoxia may be triggered by:
    a. Antihistamine use
    b. Caffeine consumption
    c. Alcohol use
    d. All of these

14. A patient who uses Pyridium may experience what changes in his or her urination?
    a. Excessive urination
    b. Lack of urination
    c. Discoloration
    d. All of the above

15. What issue might a patient have when it comes to a phlebotomy?
    a. The process is time-consuming
    b. The practice may be too expensive
    c. The patient may have a fear of needles
    d. All of these are issues

16. What should a patient with hemochromatosis avoid?
    a. Vitamin C
    b. Vitamin A
    c. Calcium
    d. Potassium

17. What is the greatest danger that carbon monoxide poses to hemoglobin?
    a. CO bonds to hemoglobin faster
    b. CO can mix with oxygen
    c. CO kills off blood cells
    d. CO does not produce any effects

18. What should a patient who has been diagnosed with PKU avoid?

a. Fruit
b. Protein
c. Juice
d. Vegetables

19. Who should not receive a flu vaccination?

a. A toddler
b. A pregnant woman
c. A 90-year-old person
d. A frequent smoker

20. What may develop due to thalassemia major?

a. Cataracts
b. Heart disease
c. Obesity
d. Diabetes

21. Iron supplementation can help with resolving minor cases of anemia. What food should also be added to a person's diet?

a. Whole grain bread
b. Green vegetables
c. Citrus fruits
d. Dairy products

22. In the Trendelenburg position, a patient is supine. How should the legs be positioned?

a. Extended
b. Together
c. Flat
d. No specific direction

23. Swelling can occur due to compartment syndrome. The swelling will result in:

a. Seizures
b. Hypertension
c. Blood flow being lost in an area
d. Nerves being damaged

24. What test should be performed when determining whether a patient is experiencing compartment syndrome?

a. An X-ray
b. An MRI
c. A CT scan
d. An arterial ultrasound

25. A patient's Glasgow Coma Scale number has dropped since being admitted to a hospital. A telemetry monitor shows a pulseless concern. What should be done at this point?

a. Conduct a CT scan of the brain
b. Administer epinephrine
c. Administer atropine
d. Insert a breathing tube

26. Which is not an actual type of blood?

a. A positive
b. AB negative
c. AO negative
d. O negative

27. Who can receive O negative blood?

a. People with O positive blood
b. People with AB positive blood
c. People with A- blood
d. Anyone can receive O negative blood

28. Which of the following is true about providing a transfusion to a patient with O positive blood?

a. Only O positive or negative blood can work
b. Only O positive blood can work
c. Only positive blood can work
d. All blood types can work in this situation

29. The best possible Glasgow Coma Scale for a patient is:

a. 6
b. 8
c. 10
d. 12

30. An air leak is found in a patient's chest tube. What should be done?
    a. Remove the tube
    b. Strip the tube
    c. Clamp the tube
    d. Apply a compound around the incision site

31. What people are at risk of developing diarrhea due to a food allergy?
    a. People with celiac disease
    b. People who are lactose intolerant
    c. Those who consume peanuts and other legumes
    d. A and B

32. When is a breath test appropriate for diagnosing diarrhea?
    a. If a person is lactose intolerant
    b. If a person is overweight
    c. If a patient has undergone recent surgery
    d. If an enema is unsafe

33. What makes whole grains part of a healthy diet?
    a. More folic acid
    b. Added zinc
    c. More fiber
    d. All of the above

34. Which of the following is true of priapism?
    a. It may develop following sex
    b. It can impact the abdomen
    c. It is not caused by sexual arousal
    d. It may cause discharge

35. What can be prescribed to reduce the intracranial pressure in a patient?
    a. Lasix
    b. Lanoxin
    c. Levothyroxine
    d. Lantus

36. What should a nurse ask about when monitoring a patient who has Guillain-Barré syndrome?

a. How easily the patient bruises
b. Family history of GBS
c. Whether the patient has traveled anywhere recently
d. Whether the person has experienced any recent infections

37. What type of testicular injury may be identified a few hours after it occurs?

a. Torsion
b. Hydrocele
c. Varicocele
d. Carcinoma

38. A hydrocele entails the following occurring in the testicle:

a. Fluid around the testicle
b. Bruising in the testicle
c. Internal bleeding
d. Sore sensation

39. What should be administered to a patient who is experiencing tachycardia without a pulse?

a. Dopamine
b. Lidocaine
c. Magnesium
d. Amiodarone

40. What should be done if a patient cannot swallow an aspirin?

a. Crush the pill
b. Double the dose later
c. Insert the pill rectally
d. Skip the aspirin dose

41. What may be observed in a case in which a patient has progressive esophageal dysphagia that entails a mechanical obstruction produced by the consumption of solid food?

a. Frequent heartburn
b. Esophageal cancer
c. Chest pains
d. A and B

42. Scleroderma may develop in a patient who has contracted esophageal dysphagia. The condition may cause chronic:

a. Respiratory issues
b. Heartburn
c. Spasms
d. All of the above

43. Which tests can be performed on a patient with dysphagia that may be triggered by the esophagus?

a. An X-ray of the region
b. A barium swallow
c. An endoscopic analysis
d. Any of the above may work

44. What is noticeable in a testicular carcinoma?

a. It is painful
b. There is a soft sensation
c. It is fixed in one spot
d. All of the above

45. A patient who has gastroesophageal reflux needs esomeprazole. What does esomeprazole do?

a. It controls digestion
b. It controls peristalsis
c. It prevents acid erosion
d. It reduces stomach acid production

46. How can NSAIDs impact the stomach?

a. They create a full feeling
b. They cause an erosion of the lining
c. They prevent the stomach from fully emptying
d. They can cause the stomach to shrink slightly

47. Inflammation in the pelvis can cause:

a. Appendicitis
b. Infertility
c. Bleeding
d. An increased potential for multiple births

48. A patient with GERD should be placed in what position in the bed?
  a. Trendelenburg
  b. Reverse Trendelenburg
  c. Fowler's
  d. Semi-Fowler's

49. What is the difference between the Fowler's and Semi-Fowler's positions?
  a. Fowler's has the head of the bed elevated at a smaller angle
  b. Fowler's has the head of the bed elevated at a larger angle
  c. Semi-Fowler's has the foot of the bed raised
  d. Semi-Fowler's has the foot of the bed lowered

50. A patient in a cervical collar should be placed in what bed position?
  a. Fowler's
  b. Flat
  c. Trendelenburg
  d. Reverse Trendelenburg

51. What is not effective in the treatment of symptoms relating to PMS?
  a. Caffeine
  b. Birth control medication
  c. Exercise
  d. Dietary changes

52. A patient with PMS may experience such effects as:
  a. Anxiety
  b. Hunger
  c. Constipation
  d. All of these are issues that are common to PMS

53. The most important part of eating a healthy diet is that it:
  a. Controls the heart rate
  b. Regulates body temperature
  c. Regulates blood sugar
  d. All of these are true

54. Cervical cancer may be prevented through:
  a. Abstinence from alcohol
  b. Not having too many sexual partners
  c. Not using diaphragms
  d. Regular testing for sexually transmitted diseases

55. Beriberi is a condition that entails a lack of:
   a. Potassium
   b. Thiamine
   c. Vitamin C
   d. Calcium

56. A patient with this body temperature (Fahrenheit) may be diagnosed as having a fever:
   a. 99.8
   b. 100.2
   c. 100.5
   d. B and C

57. Hypothermia occurs when the body temperature drops below this level:
   a. 95 F
   b. 96 F
   c. 97 F
   d. 98 F

58. Beriberi can trigger all of these conditions except for:
   a. Diabetes
   b. Muscle tears
   c. Seizures
   d. Encephalopathy

59. What should be done to reduce the risk of developing diabetes mellitus?
   a. Add iron to the diet
   b. Reduce alcohol consumption
   c. Add vitamin B1
   d. Avoid processed foods

60. What can trigger the symptoms of gout?
   a. Caffeine
   b. Sugar
   c. Dairy products
   d. Alcohol

61. The effects of anemia can be reduced by adding what to one's diet?

a. Iron
b. Calcium
c. Vitamin C
d. Vitamin B1

62. A patient who had a stroke is being discharged from a hospital and requires regular monitoring. What advice should the patient be given?

a. Increase his or her physical activities only under the guidance of a doctor
b. Consult other medical specialists as needed
c. Remain on bed rest for most of the day
d. Call 911 if there are ever any sudden changes

63. A patient who experiences a drop in blood sugar may experience:

a. Changes in mental status
b. Changes in physical activity
c. Changes in appetite
d. Seizures

64. What can occur when a patient undergoes a blood transfusion?

a. Fainting
b. Infertility
c. Hyperactivity
d. Rise in blood temperature

65. When a patient undergoing a blood transfusion develops a fever, what should be done?

a. Administer antihistamines
b. Stop the transfusion
c. Provide painkillers
d. Perform an EKG

66. What can an NSAID do for a patient's blood flow?

a. Increase bleeding risk
b. Clot the blood
c. Lower blood pressure
d. Regulate pressure

67. What can be said about a patient's rectal temperature versus an oral temperature?

a. It is lower by one degree
b. It is the same
c. It is higher by one degree
d. A rectal temperature is unhelpful

68. Which of the following is correct advice to give a patient taking warfarin?

a. Take it in the evening
b. Take it in the morning
c. Double the dose if you miss one
d. Take it without food

69. What effect does vitamin K have on warfarin?

a. Makes it stronger
b. Makes it weaker
c. Causes a toxic reaction
d. No noticeable effects

70. A patient experienced a PE. The patient needed a blood transfusion but received the wrong blood type. What may be noted in the patient?

a. Sickle cell disease
b. Transfusion reaction
c. Epistaxis
d. An allergic reaction

71. A vasospasm has developed in a patient. What should be done to prevent the condition from worsening?

a. Keep the blood pressure high
b. Apply a warm compress
c. Administer antihypertensive medicine
d. Maintain stasis

72. An ileus should be treated by:

a. Resting the patient's bowel
b. Surgical intervention
c. Providing pain medication
d. Performing a blood transfusion

73. The relationship between the nurse and client entails all but the following steps:
  a. Orientation
  b. Termination
  c. Working
  d. Resolution

74. The nurse/client relationship entails all but the following in the orientation phase:
  a. Time
  b. Trust
  c. Purpose
  d. Knowledge

75. When monitoring how a patient is responding to treatment, what should a nurse focus on?
  a. Any questions the patient asks
  b. How comfortable the patient is
  c. How irritable the patient is
  d. Whether the person refuses to cooperate

76. What should be assessed in a patient's blood sample?
  a. How hydrated it is
  b. Iron content
  c. Sugar level
  d. Any discoloration

77. A patient is receiving Pradaxa. What are some possible side effects?
  a. Coughing
  b. Bleeding
  c. Liver difficulties
  d. Toxicity

78. OBRA is designed to monitor:
  a. Medical malpractice
  b. How nursing home residents are cared for
  c. Herbal medicine treatments
  d. Medical waste handling

79. Is it safe to mix Nexium and Plavix together?
   a. Yes
   b. No
   c. Depends on the dosage
   d. Depends on the patient's condition

80. What is a symptom of Sjogren's syndrome?
   a. Dry eyes
   b. Dry mouth
   c. Swallowing difficulties
   d. All of the above

81. What can be prescribed to reduce the severity of Sjogren's syndrome?
   a. Birth control pills
   b. Albuterol
   c. Saline spray
   d. Antihistamines

82. A patient with superficial vein thrombosis should receive:
   a. An ultrasound
   b. Lovenox
   c. Rest
   d. IVCF support

83. A patient with status epilepticus should not:
   a. Have his or her airway checked for obstruction
   b. Be placed in the reverse Trendelenburg position
   c. Receive added oxygen
   d. Be prescribed benzodiazepines

84. What type of scan is recommended for a patient with a clot?
   a. An ultrasound
   b. An MRI
   c. An X-ray
   d. An electrocardiogram

85. What should be done if a patient experiences hypoxia?
   a. Increase oxygen
   b. Restore blood sugar
   c. Restore blood pressure
   d. Add supplemental oxygen

86. A patient who has anxiety states that he is claustrophobic and would struggle with an MRI. What medication can help relieve a patient's worry prior to the MRI?

a. Lorazepam
b. Lopressor
c. Lantus
d. Levoxyl

87. Lopressor helps to:

a. Reduce heart rate
b. Reduce blood sugar
c. Increase the blood's ability to take in oxygen
d. Facilitate metabolic functions

88. Asterixis appears only in the:

a. Feet
b. Head
c. Hands
d. Legs

89. Are benzodiazepines appropriate for the treatment of phobias?

a. Yes
b. No
c. Depends on the phobia
d. Depends on the patient

90. A patient with bipolar disorder should be prescribed:

a. Lexapro
b. Decadron
c. Lantus
d. Permethrin

91. What causes scabies?

a. A mite
b. A rash
c. A drug interaction
d. Alcohol consumption

92. What is an appropriate treatment for scabies?
   a. Use sedatives to ease the severity of the condition
   b. Allow the condition to resolve on its own
   c. Apply alcohol to the impacted area
   d. Wash the patient's clothes with hot water

93. What is the greatest concern pertaining to a scabies infection?
   a. It can be transmitted to other people
   b. It may cause blood vessel damage
   c. It may not be noticed for weeks
   d. It can cause dizziness

94. What can neomycin do for a patient who has an advanced form of cirrhosis?
   a. Control the risk of a secondary infection
   b. Prevent bacterial bronchitis from occurring
   c. Remove small microorganisms
   d. Destroy intestinal compounds that can produce ammonia over protein

95. A mother with B- blood has a fetus with A- blood. Is RhoGAM treatment necessary?
   a. Yes
   b. No
   c. Depends on the severity of the situation
   d. Consult another doctor for information

96. Who is at the greatest risk of harm from Rhesus disease?
   a. Mother
   b. Fetus
   c. Both
   d. Neither

97. What is an appropriate treatment for Rhesus disease?
   a. A blood transfusion to the unborn child
   b. Phototherapy after the child's birth
   c. An antibody injection after birth
   d. Any of these can work

98. What is evident in a person's neck when that person has a heart attack?

a. The neck feels tight
b. The patient keeps feeling popping
c. The person develops hearing issues
d. Nothing noticeable occurs

99. When a patient vomits while having a heart attack, what is distinctive about the vomitus?

a. All foods consumed may be expelled in the vomitus
b. Blood may appear in the vomitus
c. The vomitus is mostly solid
d. There is nothing distinct about the vomitus

100. Is it safe to do a finger sweep if a patient is choking?

a. Yes. It helps remove the obstruction
b. No. It pushes the obstruction back
c. Does not apply because the mouth may be inaccessible
d. A finger sweep is always safe

101. At what point in a pregnancy is a woman most likely to vomit?

a. During the first trimester
b. During the second trimester
c. During the third trimester
d. Never

102. Which of the following signs, accompanied by vomiting, requires immediate medical care?

a. Blood in vomit
b. Rapid actions
c. Sporadic motions
d. Twitching after vomiting

103. If a nurse accidentally sticks himself or herself with a needle during a surgical procedure, what should he or she do?

a. Discontinue working on the surgery
b. Notify the patient as soon as possible
c. Tell a supervisor
d. Clean the wound

104. Abdominal thrusts should be used when a patient is choking and:

a. There is a partial obstruction
b. There is a complete obstruction
c. The patient is not breathing
d. Abdominal thrusts are appropriate at any time

105. The prothrombin time is a measure of ___________ in plasma:

a. Pressure
b. Clotting time
c. Development
d. Drain

106. How does a patient's ear temperature compare with his or her rectal temperature?

a. The ear temperature is about one degree higher
b. The rectal temperature is one degree higher
c. It is the same
d. The ear temperature is unreliable

107. What is the best prothrombin time?

a. 10 seconds
b. 20 seconds
c. 40 seconds
d. 60 seconds

108. A patient who has hepatitis is being analyzed for asterixis. What is one of the steps a nurse should take while doing an assessment?

a. Ask the patient to squat down
b. Palpate the patient's abdomen
c. Have the patient extend his or her feet as far out as possible
d. Have the patient extend his or her arm and hand as much as possible

109. A person is choking. She can cough, but her face has a bright-red look. What procedure is necessary?

a. Abdominal thrusts
b. Back slap
c. Provide a small amount of water
d. Complete a finger sweep

110. How long should diarrhea last in an average patient?
a. 2 days
b. 5 days
c. 7 days
d. There is no set time

111. A patient is in a hospital, and his family members are there. The only orders entail admitting the patient to the surgical unit and performing tests as needed. The patient starts to have a seizure. What should a nurse not do?
a. Administer a bolus
b. Rearrange the patient's position
c. Call another physician for help
d. Tell family members to leave

112. What is a symptom of acute pancreatitis in a patient who has engaged in alcohol abuse?
a. Difficulty breathing
b. Difficult bowel movements
c. Reduced glucose
d. Chvostek's sign

113. What is a test that can be performed to confirm that yellow skin and eyes are signs of jaundice in an infant?
a. White blood cell count
b. Blood pressure test
c. Bilirubin test
d. Colic review

114. How much of the liver can potentially regrow?
a. At least 25 percent
b. At least half of the liver
c. Most of the liver
d. The liver cannot regrow

115. How long does it take for the liver to regain its original weight after a surgical procedure or other infection that weakens the organ?
a. 2 days
b. 5 days
c. 10 days
d. A month

116. A patient who frequently experiences acid reflux should avoid:
   a. Wine
   b. Oatmeal
   c. Tea
   d. Sorghum

117. A person who has gallbladder disease can develop pancreatitis. As part of treatment, what should the patient be advised to do?
   a. Ensure consistent ambulation
   b. Consume milk frequently
   c. Place a heating pad over the area
   d. Remain lying down

118. Bilirubin levels are critical for the body's functionality. What is bilirubin?
   a. A material excreted by white blood cells
   b. A substance that lubricates the kidneys
   c. A compound produced by red blood cells breaking down
   d. A compound that supports the regrowth of the liver

119. Should chemotherapy be performed after a cancer patient is in remission?
   a. If possible
   b. Never
   c. Depends on the cancer
   d. Depends on the location of the cancer

120. Who is more likely to experience a foreign body in the digestive system?
   a. Children
   b. Patients with mental disorders
   c. Senior citizens
   d. A and B

121. What can be used to confirm a hernia in a patient?
   a. A CT scan
   b. An ultrasound
   c. A lumbar puncture
   d. An EKG

122. Hepatitis A can be contracted through:
- a. Contact with other people's fluids
- b. The presence of hepatitis B
- c. Water or food consumption
- d. Sexual activity

123. Which of the following is true of tracheitis?
- a. It can develop in children
- b. It occurs in obese patients
- c. It can last for months at a time
- d. It may damage the esophagus

124. What can be said about the pleural fluid in a patient who has experienced pleural effusion?
- a. There is no specific total for how much fluid there may be
- b. There will be a very small amount of fluid
- c. There will be an excessive amount of fluid
- d. The amount of fluid will keep fluctuating

125. What may happen if a contusion occurs in the lung?
- a. A patient may experience a rise in body temperature
- b. A patient may experience fatigue
- c. The alveoli may swell and collect blood
- d. A patient may start to breathe rapidly

126. What part of the artery includes the smooth muscle fibers?
- a. Tunica externa
- b. Tunica media
- c. Muscular tissue
- d. Arteriole

127. What makes a superficial vein different from other veins?
- a. It appears near the skin's surface
- b. It is surrounded by other arteries
- c. It is near the right atrium
- d. It handles oxygen

128. A baby has a body temperature of 100 degrees Fahrenheit. Is this safe?
   a. Yes
   b. No
   c. Depends on the baby's age
   d. Depends on the baby's blood type

129. Diverticulitis is more likely to occur among people who are:
   a. Younger
   b. Older
   c. Experiencing celiac issues
   d. Dealing with Crohn's

130. What test should be administered when seeking the cause for non-menstrual vaginal bleeding?
   a. A CBC test
   b. A hormonal assay
   c. A Pap smear
   d. All of the above

131. Who should not use fluconazole?
   a. Pregnant women
   b. Women in menopause
   c. Women who have experienced non-menstrual vaginal bleeding
   d. Fluconazole is safe for all

132. A boric acid capsule may be inserted into the vagina to control the bacteria that triggers a vaginal yeast infection. Is it safe for a patient to orally consume a boric acid capsule?
   a. Always
   b. Never
   c. Depends on if a doctor recommends it
   d. Depends on if the woman is pregnant

133. A focal seizure is unique for occurring:
   a. Only in one part of the brain
   b. In all parts of the brain
   c. Near the brain
   d. A focal seizure is not unique

134. What may be noticed in a tonic seizure?
   a. Shaking
   b. Loss of bowel control
   c. Facial spasms
   d. B and C

135. How can diabetes cause incontinence to develop?
   a. It weakens the bladder
   b. It damages the nerves
   c. It causes a lack of blood flow
   d. Diabetes can cause all of the above, which can lead to incontinence

136. How long does it take for the effects of a spinal cord injury to be fully evident?
   a. Effects are evident immediately
   b. Effects are evident in 24 to 48 hours
   c. Effects are evident in about a week
   d. Effects are evident in about a month

137. How can lowering a patient's body temperature help treat a spinal cord injury?
   a. It facilitates the regrowth of nerves
   b. It prevents cellular death
   c. It does not help treat a spinal cord injury
   d. A and B

138. What can cause a flail chest to develop?
   a. Fractured ribs
   b. Punctured lung
   c. Excess fluid
   d. All of the above

139. What treatment is appropriate when treating a diaphragm injury?
   a. The Heimlich maneuver
   b. Surgery
   c. Antibiotics
   d. A bronchoscopy

140. Oxygenated blood moves through the body via the:
   a. Arteries
   b. Capillaries
   c. Arterioles
   d. Aorta

141. What makes the posterior arteries critical to the health of the Circle of Willis?
   a. They move blood to the lungs
   b. They help blood move through the heart
   c. They carry oxygenated blood
   d. They facilitate the growth of white blood cells

142. Endocarditis is a condition in which the heart becomes:
   a. Inflamed
   b. Irritated
   c. Weakened
   d. Sore

143. When is a pericardiectomy necessary?
   a. When the pericardium has a tear
   b. When the pericardium becomes too rigid
   c. When the pericardium is leaking
   d. When the pericardium is not taking in blood well enough

144. Which of the following is true about delirium?
   a. Delirium can occur anywhere
   b. Delirium occurs suddenly
   c. Delirium can be influenced by personal events
   d. Seniors are more likely to experience delirium

145. What should be assessed in a patient who has experienced a possible case of sexual assault?
   a. Injuries to the body
   b. Penetration
   c. Bloodstains
   d. All of the above

146. What is the first test that should be performed on a woman who has been sexually assaulted?
   a. A CT scan
   b. A Pap smear
   c. A pregnancy test
   d. An MRI

147. The supine position requires all but the following:
   a. Pillows on the sides
   b. A pillow under the shoulders
   c. Keeping the legs upright
   d. Head support

148. The later position requires a patient to lie on:
   a. The side
   b. The back
   c. The front
   d. The patient should remain upright

149. Which blood type can a person who has AB+ donate blood to?
   a. AB+
   b. A+
   c. O+
   d. Any of these

150. What type of blood can a patient who has O+ blood receive in a transfusion?
   a. O+
   b. B+
   c. A-
   d. AB-

Test 2 Answers

1. **c.** Twitching can be observed when Chvostek's sign occurs. The twitching happens when blood pressure changes occur.

2. **a.** Hypemic hypoxia occurs when the blood cannot carry oxygen. Answer B entails hypoxic hypoxia, a condition in which the patient cannot get enough oxygen due to being at a high altitude or other place where oxygen is not readily available.

3. **d.** All of these parts should be monitored. A person with hemochromatosis will have an excess amount of iron in all of these areas. The heart should also be monitored.

4. **b.** The liver is the first organ to be impacted by blood-related concerns. Since the liver manages toxins, there is a possibility it could be damaged.

5. **c.** The patient is experiencing alcohol intoxication. A CT scan will not show anything of note. The patient's slurring of words may also be a concern.

6. **d.** Any of those numbers would be an appropriate alcohol level for a patient. The patient's alcohol level should be under 10.

7. **d.** A bolus administers a medication within a specific time frame. This includes letting medication work in about 30 minutes, as it may require time for a condition to develop before the treatment can be effective.

8. **a.** Lanoxin is appropriate for the treatment of atrial fibrillation and other heart rhythm-related issues. The medication is an antiarrhythmic compound.

9. **d.** Cerebrospinal fluid is not produced as much when the transport of sodium is affected through the use of Lasix or other diuretics, especially ones that prevent cerebral edema.

10. **c.** The nurse should assess the patient's consciousness last. The airways and breathing should be examined first. This procedure ensures the patient's most important vital signs are assessed at the start.

11. **a.** Jaundice can develop in a person who uses Pyridium. Other side effects include weakness, confusion and pale skin.

12. **c.** A mountain climber is more likely to experience hypoxia, as mountain climbing may entail reaching higher altitudes where oxygen may be scarce.

13. **c.** Alcohol use can trigger histotoxic hypoxia. The condition occurs when the cells that usually receive oxygen are impaired.

14. **d.** All of the above problems are urination-related risks triggered by Pyridium use. A patient may experience more or less urination, not to mention an unusual color in his or her urine. All urination-related problems will resolve when the patient no longer requires Pyridium.

15. **c.** A fear of needles may be present in some patients since the phlebotomy process involves drawing blood. The practice is common and does not take much time, so A and B are both wrong.

16. **a.** Vitamin C should be avoided among patients with hemochromatosis. Patients with the condition have more iron than necessary. Vitamin C helps increase the body's ability to absorb iron, thus making the vitamin dangerous and inappropriate for patients with hemochromatosis.

17. **a.** CO bonds to hemoglobin faster, thus making it harder for the hemoglobin to carry out its usual functions.

18. **b.** Patients with PKU should avoid amino acids found in proteins that are difficult for the body to break down.

19. **a.** A toddler does not require the flu vaccine. A child should be at least six months of age to receive it. Those who are pregnant, elderly or have weak immune systems should get the vaccine.

20. **b.** Heart disease can develop due to thalassemia major. The hemoglobin in the blood will not perform its usual functions, thus resulting in anemia. The condition will result in heart disease due to the blood not flowing properly.

21. **c.** Citrus fruits are appropriate for when a patient needs added iron. Citrus fruits have more vitamin C in them, which makes it easier for the body to absorb iron.

22. **a.** The legs should be extended to allow blood to flow to the heart and other areas.

23. **c.** Blood flow will be lost in the area where compartment syndrome is present. The tissue may die off if the blood flow is not restored soon.

24. **d.** An arterial ultrasound is necessary to diagnose compartment syndrome.

25. **d.** The doctor should insert a breathing tube into the patient. The airway should be supported, and the patient's breathing should then be assessed. Circulation can be assessed after that.

26. **c.** AO negative is not an actual blood type. The blood types are A, B, O or AB, and are always positive or negative.

27. **d.** Anyone can receive O negative blood. This is the only blood type that is universally compatible.

28. **c.** Only positive blood is appropriate to transfuse into a patient with O positive blood. The positive forms of A, B, O and AB blood are acceptable in this case.

29. **d.** 12 is the best GCS score in the answers provided. A patient with a GCS of 8 or under would be comatose. The best possible GCS is 15.

30. **c.** The nurse should clamp the tube. Stripping the tube would damage it, while an adhesive may be too painful and may not work as well.

31. **d.** The first two answers are correct. A patient with celiac disease or lactose intolerance can develop diarrhea. A patient who has a peanut or legume sensitivity will not develop diarrhea but can experience a more significant concern like breathing difficulties that may become fatal.

32. **a.** A breath test may be used to diagnose diarrhea if a person is lactose intolerant. The test may identify changes in a person's breath, including whether there are noticeable lactose particles in it.

33. **d.** All of the above answers are correct about whole grains. Unlike white grains, whole grains contain more fiber, zinc, magnesium, chromium and folic acid. They stimulate the colon.

34. **c.** Priapism is not caused by sexual arousal. It may be triggered by blood difficulties, blood pressure changes or an injury in the area.

35. **a.** Lasix should help to reduce the intracranial pressure. The medication moves fluid from the cranial area and back into circulation, thus easing tension in the area.

36. **d.** The patient should be asked about whether he or she has had any recent infections. GBS does not have a specific cause that can be pinpointed, although an immune response may be a threat.

37. **a.** Torsion may be evident a few hours after it takes place and can cause significant harm if not swiftly treated.

38. **a.** Fluid may develop around the testicle due to a hydrocele.

39. **a.** Dopamine is recommended to boost a patient's heart rate.

40. **c.** The medication can be inserted rectally. Food should not be provided along with the aspirin, as it might cause aspiration. The patient should not skip the aspirin dosage, nor should he or she take more than the necessary total in a dosage.

41. **d.** Frequent heartburn and esophageal cancer may develop, although the specific condition may vary based on a person's age. A patient at least 50 years of age will be more likely to experience esophageal cancer. Heartburn can occur regardless of the patient's age.

42. **b.** Heartburn can trigger scleroderma in cases in which a patient develops dysphagia from both solid and liquid foods. The condition may occur due to a progressive neuromuscular disorder.

43. **b.** A barium swallow helps to identify dysphagia triggered by the esophagus.

44. **c.** A testicular carcinoma is fixed in one spot. A and B are incorrect, as the carcinoma is painless and will feel hard.

45. **d.** Esomeprazole will reduce stomach acid production. The medication works better than an NSAID. Esomeprazole is a proton pump inhibitor that prompts the stomach to produce less stomach acid, thereby preventing damage.

46. **b.** NSAIDs can cause erosion in the lining of the stomach. This can cause GERD to become more severe.

47. **b.** Inflammation of the pelvis can cause infertility. Gonorrhea, chlamydia and other sexually transmitted diseases that cause inflammation may be factors. Such conditions can all potentially cause infertility.

48. **b.** The reverse Trendelenburg position is ideal because the patient's airway will be open and easier to maintain.

49. **b.** In the Fowler's position the head of the bed is elevated to 45 degrees versus the 30 degrees in the Semi-Fowler's position.

50. **d.** The reverse Trendelenburg position is ideal for a patient who is in a cervical collar. The head remains upright, protecting it from injury.

51. **a.** Caffeine will not relieve the symptoms of PMS. Caffeine can actually trigger cramping and food cravings, thus making PMS worse.

52. **d.** All of these effects are common side effects of PMS. A patient can develop anxiety, appetite changes, fatigue, constipation or diarrhea, nausea and/or gas.

53. **c.** A healthy diet regulates blood sugar. By keeping blood sugar levels in check, a person will not feel excess food cravings. Mood swings will not develop due to blood sugar levels being too high or low.

54. **b.** The patient should not have too many sexual partners. Cervical cancer can be triggered by HPV, which can be transmitted through sex. Fewer sexual partners lessen the risk of transmission.

55. **b.** Beriberi entails a lack of thiamine, or vitamin B1. The condition may be triggered by a poor diet or by excess alcohol consumption.

56. **c.** 100.5 degrees may be interpreted as a fever. A fever is considered to start at 100.4 degrees.

57. **a.** A patient whose body temperature drops below 95 degrees will be diagnosed with hypothermia. The patient should receive appropriate treatment as quickly as possible in order to prevent complications.

58. **a.** Beriberi does not trigger diabetes. It can cause nerve damage, which is something that does occur with diabetic patients.

59. **d.** A person can prevent diabetes mellitus by lessening his or her consumption of processed foods, thereby avoiding excessive sugar consumption.

60. **d.** Alcohol will trigger the symptoms of gout. The other three may contribute to gout symptoms, but they do not trigger them as much as alcohol can.

61. **a.** Iron should be added to a person's diet to reduce the effects of anemia. Iron is necessary for the formation of healthy red blood cells.

62. **a.** The patient should not be on bed rest most of the day. Regular physical activity is encouraged to help the patient recover more quickly.

63. **a.** There may be changes in a patient's mental status due to a drop in blood sugar.

64. **a.** Fainting may occur during a blood transfusion. This is a result of receiving blood from a new source. Fainting is normal in this case.

65. **b.** The nurse must stop the transfusion before any of the other solutions can be utilized to resolve the problem.

66. **a.** NSAIDs can increase a patient's bleeding risk. An NSAID can work in the same way as an antiplatelet agent when resolving clotting-related issues.

67. **c.** A rectal temperature measurement is about one degree higher on average than the oral temperature. A rectal temperature exam is appropriate in cases in which the patient is incapable of keeping a thermometer in his or her mouth.

68. **a.** It is best for a patient to take warfarin in the evening. A patient should never double a dose if he or she misses one. It is also recommended that a patient take warfarin with food in order to assist with absorption.

69. **b.** Vitamin K can weaken warfarin. Green tea and various other components that contain vitamin K should be avoided for the patient's safety.

70. **b.** A transfusion reaction will be noticed at this point.

71. **a.** A patient with a vasospasm should keep his or her blood pressure high in order to maintain hydration in the body.

72. **a.** An ileus can be treated by resting a patient's bowels. The patient should not take any food by mouth. Sips of liquids are fine. The limitations allow the bowel to normally contract, thus allowing waste to move out of the body.

73. **d.** The resolution stage is not a part of the nurse-client relationship. The relationship goes through the pre-interaction, orientation, working and termination phases.

74. **d.** Knowledge is not a part of the orientation phase in the nurse/client relationship. The client is not expected to know everything the nurse does. The orientation phase focuses on the purpose of the meeting, the nature of the work and the trust between parties.

75. **d.** The nurse should take note if the person refuses to cooperate. Although there is a potential for all of the scenarios in these answer choices to develop, a person might not want to follow through on what the nurse recommends. The patient should be clearly advised as to why certain steps are necessary for the treatment process.

76. **b.** The iron level should be assessed. An iron overload may develop if a patient receives blood that has far too much iron in it. This overload can harm the liver and heart.

77. **b.** Bleeding can occur due to Pradaxa use. This is due to Pradaxa being a blood thinner.

78. **b.** OBRA monitors how nursing home residents are cared for. The Omnibus Budget Reconciliation Act requires that all nursing homes implement proper safety measures in order to allow patients to go about their daily activities without fear of harm.

79. **b.** Nexium and Plavix should never be mixed under any circumstance. Nexium blocks an enzyme that will allow Plavix to work in its active form.

80. **d.** All of the above issues are a result of Sjogren's syndrome. The salivary and tear glands will be impacted, thus causing dryness and making it harder for a person to eat.

81. **c.** Saline spray may help with resolving the symptoms of Sjogren's syndrome, such as dry eyes.

82. **b.** Lovenox should be administered to resolve the superficial vein thrombosis issue. Coumadin may also be prescribed if the patient's risk is significantly higher. Resting is not advisable, as it might make the patient's condition worse.

83. **a.** Checking the mouth for an obstruction is not recommended as, if a patient is seizing, it may not even be possible to safely perform such an assessment.

84. **a.** An ultrasound can identify the clot, whether or not the clot is moving and any changes that have taken place.

85. **d.** The nurse should provide supplemental oxygen if the patient experiences hypoxia. This is a condition in which the body is not receiving enough oxygen.

86. **a.** Lorazepam may be prescribed before the MRI. Lorazepam works as a benzodiazepine, making it useful for the treatment of anxiety.

87. **a.** Lopressor reduces the patient's heart rate. Lopressor works as a treatment for hypertension, heart failure and other conditions that cause the heart to become dangerously overactive.

88. **c.** Asterixis appears only in the hands. A person with asterixis will flap his or her hands constantly.

89. **a.** Benzodiazepines are appropriate for the treatment of phobias. Such medications sedate patients, thus relieving their tension.

90. **a.** Lexapro is ideal for bipolar disorder. The medication treats various psychiatric concerns, including cases in which a patient's mood may fluctuate.

91. **a.** A mite is likely to trigger scabies. The mite may burrow into the patient's skin and produce an itching sensation. A rash will also develop.

92. **d.** The patient's clothes should be washed with hot water. The heat can kill off the scabies infection and any mites that might trigger the condition.

93. **c.** A scabies infection may not be noticed for weeks. It can take a few weeks for the scabies infection to appear after the mite enters the patient's body and starts burrowing.

94. **d.** Neomycin destroys intestinal compounds that can produce ammonia over protein. The medication will not enter the patient's circulation, but it will help to restore the body's functionality.

95. **a.** A RhoGAM treatment is necessary to prevent immune responses to Rh+ blood in people with Rh- blood.

96. **b.** The fetus is at risk of harm due to Rhesus disease as the mother's blood cells will destroy the unborn baby's blood cells.

97. **d.** All three of the options can work. The blood transfusion prior to birth is only for the most significant cases. The other two treatments can be administered right after birth and when the baby appears to show signs of jaundice.

98. **a.** The neck feels tight when the patient is having a heart attack. A general sense of discomfort may also occur. The neck irritation can spread to the arms.

99. **a.** Any foods consumed may be expelled when vomiting. There will not be distinct changes in the vomitus, nor will there be any blood. The vomiting should be confirmed alongside general chest pains and breathlessness.

100. **b.** A finger sweep may push the obstruction back. This makes it harder to remove and is therefore not an advisable treatment.

101. **a.** The first trimester is when a woman is more likely to vomit.

102. **a.** Blood in vomit is often a sign of a more significant concern, such as internal bleeding.

103. **a.** The nurse must stop working on the surgery if he or she is stuck by a needle. The wound must be cleaned. The nurse should then report to an emergency department for immediate testing to identify what steps need to be taken next.

104. **b.** Abdominal thrusts work when there is a complete obstruction in the airway.

105. **b.** The clotting time is measured in a prothrombin time test. The measure is based on how well the plasma helps to prevent bleeding.

106. **c.** The ear temperature is the same as the rectal temperature. The ear temperature is for cases in which a patient cannot hold a thermometer in his or her mouth. The ear readout may also be faster and could provide a more accurate readout.

107. **a.** 10 seconds is the ideal prothrombin time. A patient's time should be from 10 to 15 seconds. This means that the patient's blood will clot in enough time to prevent bleeding episodes from occurring.

108. **d.** The patient should extend his or her arm and hand as much as possible. Asterixis entails a hand tremor. It may be difficult for someone with asterixis to fully extend an arm or hand.

109. **c.** A small amount of water may be provided to the patient. Water can help clear the patient's throat.

110. **d.** Any of these time frames are fine. Diarrhea should last for only a week at the most.

111. **a.** The nurse should not administer a bolus. The nurse should contact a physician or other practitioner to prepare the bolus. The other solutions are fine. It is best to tell family members to leave in order to avoid distractions while treating the patient.

112. **d.** Chvostek's sign can be noted through twitching and other actions. The facial nerve should be tapped to confirm the diagnosis.

113. **c.** A bilirubin test can confirm that the issue is jaundice.

114. **a.** At least 25 percent of the liver must be present in order for it to regrow. The liver is capable of regrowing after surgery or chemical damage.

115. **c.** It takes about 10 days for the liver to regrow.

116. **a.** A patient with acid reflux should avoid wine, as wine is acidic and can cause irritation to the esophagus.

117. **d.** The patient should be encouraged to lie down. The knees should be bent slightly to provide additional pain relief.

118. **c.** Bilirubin is a compound produced by red blood cells breaking down. It has an orange-like appearance. The compound is processed in the liver and is then eliminated from the body.

119. **a.** Chemotherapy is encouraged after a cancer treatment to remove any remaining cancer cells.

120. **d.** Children and patients with mental disorders are more likely to have foreign bodies in their digestive systems. This is because neither of these two groups of people may have an awareness of the harm that can occur from swallowing a foreign body not intended for human consumption.

121. **a.** A CT scan is recommended to assess hernia.

122. **c.** Hepatitis A is contracted when a person consumes food or water contaminated with the fecal matter of a person who has the virus.

123. **a.** Tracheitis develops in children for the most part. It is an upper respiratory infection that occurs in the trachea.

124. **c.** There is an excessive amount of the pleural fluid in a person who experiences effusion. The total would entail 10ml or more of the fluid in the patient's body.

125. **c.** The alveoli in the lung will swell and collect blood, thereby causing breathing difficulties. The patient may go into shock.

126. **b.** The tunica media includes the smooth muscle fibers. These fibers help facilitate the healthy flow of blood in the artery.

127. **a.** A superficial vein appears near the skin's surface. The vein does not go near any other artery.

128. **a.** It is safe for a baby to have a body temperature of 100 degrees. A healthy body temperature for a baby is from 97.9 to 100.4 degrees Fahrenheit. This is different from the 97- to 99-degree total that a healthy adult should have.

129. **b.** Older people are more likely to experience diverticulitis. The condition occurs within the large intestine wall and can be caused by bowel pressure and other commonplace threats.

130. **d.** All of these tests are appropriate to use when assessing non-menstrual vaginal bleeding.

131. **a.** Pregnant women should not use fluconazole, as the medication may impact the unborn child.

132. **b.** A boric acid capsule should never be consumed orally. Boric acid can be deadly if swallowed.

133. **a.** A focal seizure occurs in one part of the brain. It is the opposite of a generalized seizure, which occurs in all parts of the brain.

134. **d.** Facial spasms and a loss of bowel function can occur. While facial spasms are more prominent in a tonic seizure than a loss of bowel control, there is the potential for both of these issues to occur.

135. **b.** The damage to nerves in the area can cause incontinence to develop.

136. **b.** It takes about 24 to 48 hours for the effects of a spinal cord injury to become fully noticeable. The area may continue to develop inflammation and other issues, thus making it harder to dictate the significance of the injury in a short time period.

137. **d.** Lowering the patient's body temperature will facilitate the regrowth of nerves and prevent cellular death. The sooner the treatment is administered, the better the chances the patient has for a full recovery.

138. **a.** Fractured ribs can cause a flail chest to develop.

139. **b.** Surgery is required for a diaphragm injury. Antibiotics are not always necessary, although they may be prescribed after surgery.

140. **a.** The arteries transport oxygenated blood from the heart to other parts of the body. The pulmonary vein moves blood that needs to be oxygenated.

141. **b.** The posterior arteries help blood move through the heart.

142. **a.** Endocarditis is an inflammation in the heart. The "-itis" suffix always means "inflammation."

143. **b.** A pericardiectomy should be performed only if the patient's pericardium becomes too rigid. At this point, the pericardium must be removed to allow the heart to remain flexible and to continue pumping blood as normal.

144. **b.** Delirium occurs suddenly. It involves confusion and disorientation.

145. **d.** All of these concerns should be noted when it comes to a sexual assault. These include injuries caused by vaginal penetration, traces of blood or semen and other injuries.

146. **c.** A pregnancy test should be performed. This is necessary in case the woman wants to terminate the pregnancy or requires an abortion because her own health is at risk.

147. **c.** The legs do not have to be upright in the supine position. The position is intended to make it easier for a patient to recover from a surgical procedure.

148. **a.** The patient has to be on his or her side. The top leg is in the front, while support is added beneath the head.

149. **a.** A person with AB+ blood can donate blood only to other people who have AB+ blood. The AB+ blood type is the least common one, not to mention the one that is least compatible.

150. **a.** A patient with O+ blood can receive O+ blood or O- blood. However, no other forms of blood can be utilized.

Test 3 Questions

1. What is an appropriate step to take if a patient is struggling to complete a swallow test?
   a. Use a liquid diet
   b. Use a pureed diet
   c. Use a feeding tube
   d. Continue to evaluate the patient

2. How is an appendectomy performed?
   a. With a laparoscope
   b. Through an open incision
   c. With ultrasonic waves
   d. A and B

3. Which segment of the spinal column is the closest to the skull?
   a. T11
   b. L1
   c. C2
   d. C6

4. A patient is eating food and then deliberating vomiting it back up again. This behavioral pattern is consistent. This patient is suffering from:
   a. Bulimia nervosa
   b. Anorexia nervosa
   c. Anxiety disorder
   d. Any of these conditions match the symptoms described

5. A patient has been experiencing mood swings including depression and euphoria. Which of the following is the patient suffering from?
   a. Anxiety disorder
   b. Schizophrenia
   c. Bipolar disorder
   d. Any of the above may apply

6. Which is not one of the segments in the spinal cord?
   a. Cervical
   b. Thoracic
   c. Fragmental
   d. Lumbar

7. What causes a generalized anxiety disorder to develop?
   a. There is no known reason why a person is anxious
   b. Mood swings can cause the disorder to develop
   c. Medication use can cause the disorder to develop
   d. Traumatic experiences can cause the disorder to develop

8. What can cause a bone to become infected?
   a. A fracture
   b. Blood contamination
   c. Surgery
   d. All of the above

9. Where is osteomyelitis more likely to occur?
   a. In the skull
   b. In the legs
   c. In the chest
   d. In the pelvis

10. A patient has undergone a lumbar puncture and is experiencing a headache. What position should the patient be placed in to prevent the headache from becoming worse?
   a. Sitting
   b. Trendelenburg
   c. Fowler's
   d. Supine

11. A patient who is experiencing tachycardia should be administered what medication?
   a. Morphine
   b. Adenosine
   c. Tylenol
   d. Norvasc

12. A patient has been prescribed morphine for pain relief. Which of the following is true about what he or she should do with the medication?
   a. Take as directed
   b. Take only when the pain is severe
   c. Avoid alcohol consumption
   d. Check the expiration date

13. A patient with an injury to the thoracic nerves in the spinal column will experience paralysis to the:
 a. Abdominal muscles
 b. Wrists
 c. Head and neck
 d. Biceps

14. What can the NANDA-I system be used to assess?
 a. Intervention efforts
 b. Treatment plans
 c. Patient reviews
 d. Diagnostic efforts

15. What does it mean when a person has a Stroke Scale Score of 35?
 a. The patient had a severe stroke
 b. The patient had a TIA
 c. The patient had a minor stroke
 d. The patient has a history of prior strokes

16. Digoxin is appropriate for the treatment of:
 a. Blood pressure
 b. Blood sugar
 c. Heart failure
 d. All of the above

17. Amiodarone does what for the heart?
 a. Resolves heart rhythm issues
 b. Lowers blood pressure
 c. Increases blood pressure
 d. Regulates blood sugar

18. Total parenteral nutrition entails feeding that:
 a. Does not involve the GI tract
 b. Includes fluids
 c. Involves a liquid-only diet
 d. Requires whole grains

19. A patient is having a hard time lifting his or her foot following a significant brain injury. Which of the following procedures can help this patient?

a. Elevate the foot's position
b. Use a compression stocking
c. Massage the foot
d. Use an orthopedic brace

20. A complete spinal cord injury may result in:

a. A patient retaining some sensation in the body
b. A patient losing sensation in a specific part of the body
c. The entire spinal column being affected
d. Inflammation developing around the ends of the spinal column

21. Osteopenia may also be called:

a. Excess bone growth
b. Bone spurs
c. Bone fracture
d. Bone loss

22. A patient is asking about how he or she can restore bone mass. What should the nurse advise?

a. Consume more fluids
b. Wear thicker materials
c. Eat more calcium
d. Avoid red meat consumption

23. A patient is feeling pain in the costovertebral angle. This could be a sign of:

a. Cholecystitis
b. Appendicitis
c. Bowel obstruction
d. Pyelonephritis

24. Signs of Reynolds' pentad include:

a. Wheezing and coughing
b. Confusion
c. Vomiting and weight loss
d. Skin lesions and fever

25. Reynolds' pentad is triggered by:
  a. Hypotension
  b. Hypoglycemia
  c. Hypertension
  d. Hyperglycemia

26. What is the greatest risk when it comes to heparin use?
  a. It changes the body's blood pressure
  b. It may trigger the destruction of white blood cells
  c. It causes bleeding
  d. It lowers blood sugar

27. When is Coumadin best for the treatment of a thrombus?
  a. When the patient has high blood pressure
  b. When there are multiple clots
  c. At any time
  d. Never

28. What should a patient be advised to do after a surgical procedure?
  a. Avoid fatty foods
  b. Eat as often as necessary
  c. Add more sugar to his or her diet
  d. All of the above

29. What is the purpose of Zofran?
  a. To prevent vomiting
  b. To restore blood pressure
  c. To ease cold symptoms
  d. To stop heartburn

30. Can a warm compress help with the treatment of a blood clot?
  a. It can if the clot is not dissolving
  b. It can if a medication is used at the same time
  c. It cannot help at all
  d. It can help if a secondary infection occurs

31. Which of the following should a patient with cystic fibrosis avoid?
  a. Emollients
  b. Colace
  c. Motrin
  d. Permethrin

32. A Mantoux test can identify:

a. Herpes
b. Sarcoma
c. Emphysema
d. Tuberculosis

33. The India ink test helps to identify:

a. Parasites
b. Any inflammatory infections
c. White blood cell count
d. Any organisms that have entered the body

35. A patient is threatening to commit suicide. What should a nurse not do in response to this verbalized threat?

a. Provide a psychiatric referral
b. Ask the patient to contact a suicide prevention hotline
c. Avoid reporting him or her due to confidentiality laws
d. Tell the patient's significant others

36. Calorimetry can identify:

a. How cold the body is
b. Reflex responses
c. Changes in heart activity
d. Heat produced

37. What should a patient with a long leg cast avoid doing?

a. Completing self-care activities on his or her own
b. Engaging in fast-motion activities
c. Engaging in physical therapy sessions
d. Ambulating without assistance

38. What is an ideal HbA1c test score?

a. 3
b. 5
c. 8
d. 10

39. What can worsen abdominal pain?

a. Heat
b. Activity
c. Food
d. All of the above

40. A patient may be diagnosed as having diabetes if that patient has a fasting blood glucose total of:

a. Under 100
b. Over 126
c. Between 100 and 126
d. There is no specific number that means a person is officially diabetic

41. A patient with a body mass index of 27 can be considered:

a. Underweight
b. At the ideal weight
c. Somewhat overweight
d. Obese

42. A patient has a superficial vein thrombus in an upper extremity. Which of the following is an appropriate treatment for the condition?

a. Administering Coumadin
b. Administering Lovenox
c. Applying compression
d. Adding heat

43. Thalassemia major can be treated by all of the following things except:

a. A lumbar puncture
b. A blood transfusion
c. A folate treatment
d. Chelation therapy

44. Cushing syndrome is a result of overexposure to what hormone?

a. Adrenaline
b. Cortisol
c. Testosterone
d. Dopamine

45. Acromegaly develops due to:
   a. Excess HGH
   b. Excess cortisol
   c. Lack of adrenaline
   d. Lack of testosterone

46. Cushing disease may be caused by all but the following:
   a. Tumor
   b. Steroid drug use
   c. Adrenal gland activity
   d. Hyperglycemia

47. A patient suffering from alcohol intoxication should not be prescribed:
   a. Folate
   b. Ativan
   c. Thiamine
   d. Zofran

48. What food is ideal for the treatment of acid reflux?
   a. Green leafy vegetables
   b. Tea
   c. Whole grains
   d. All of the above

49. Which of the following is not appropriate for the treatment of pneumothorax?
   a. A warm compress
   b. Administering oxygen
   c. Administering narcotics
   d. Inserting a chest tube

50. Which of the following is used to monitor intraocular pressure?
   a. Calorimetry
   b. Tonometry
   c. Spirometry
   d. Fluorescein

51. A patient who is under a total parenteral nutrition routine may be at risk of developing:
a. Alkalosis
b. Acidosis
c. Hypoglycemia
d. Hyperphosphatemia

52. A patient who has been using intravenous drugs and has hepatitis B will experience difficulty breathing and ascites. What is an appropriate treatment for this patient?
a. Nasopharyngeal suction
b. Moving the patient to a supine position
c. Keeping the patient from consuming excess fat
d. Restricting sodium consumption

53. What position should a patient with ascites be placed in?
a. Fowler's
b. Supine
c. Prone
d. Trendelenburg

54. A patient is to be treated under a CMO standard. What medication should be provided to manage the effects of tachycardia?
a. Digoxin
b. Lopressor
c. Morphine
d. Amiodarone

55. Which of the following is the most common concern noted after a cholecystectomy is performed?
a. Weak appetite
b. Abdominal pain
c. Difficulty urinating
d. Pain when coughing or sneezing

56. Prior to performing surgery on a patient for a bowel obstruction, which of the following is an appropriate step to take?
a. TPN
b. Acquiring consent
c. Replacing electrolytes
d. Providing ileostomy care

57. A patient claims to have AIDS, but that person has never been checked for the condition. What test should be used to confirm the diagnosis?

a. India ink
b. Western blot
c. Mantoux
d. RPR

58. A patient being treated for pancreatitis should be monitored for:

a. Hypercalcemia
b. ARDS
c. Pericarditis
d. Diabetes

59. What test is appropriate for diagnosing whether a patient has diabetes mellitus?

a. Cortisol
b. CBC
c. HbA1c
d. Thyroid test

60. A patient who has liver cancer is suffering from great discomfort. What should be prescribed to him or her?

a. Red blood cells
b. Vitamin K
c. Heparin
d. Protamine sulfate

61. Which of the following is most likely to trigger Hashimoto's disease in a patient?

a. Autoimmune concerns
b. Hormonal changes
c. Inactivity
d. Cancer growths

62. Is it possible to cure Hashimoto's disease?

a. Yes, through medication
b. Yes, through surgery
c. No, not in any case
d. No, but symptoms may be alleviated

63. Which of the following may be used to diagnose osteomyelitis?

a. An MRI
b. An X-ray
c. An EKG
d. An ultrasound

64. A pregnant woman has Rh-negative blood, and her child is also Rh-negative. This is her first child. Which of the following is an appropriate treatment for the woman?

a. RhoGAM
b. Ultrasound
c. Antibiotic treatment
d. Nothing is necessary

65. A patient has an A blood type, but the blood does not have the Rh factor. Therefore, the patient's blood is:

a. A-
b. A+
c. AB-
d. AB+

66. What does RhoGAM do to the immune system?

a. It accelerates the immune system in a pregnant mother
b. It suppresses the pregnant mother's immune system
c. It restores the white blood cell count in the immune system
d. It suspends the production of white blood cells

67. What is an appropriate treatment for avoiding complications from trichomoniasis?

a. Using birth control medications
b. Abstaining from sex
c. Avoiding uncooked foods
d. Avoiding alcohol use

68. A patient has an intracerebral hemorrhage. There is some edema building up around the brain. What IV fluid may be administered as part of treatment for the condition?

a. D5W
b. NaCl
c. Saline
d. Ringer's

69. A woman has developed uterine fibroids. Which of these medications should not be prescribed, as they will worsen the condition?

a. Iron pills
b. Birth control medications
c. NSAIDs
d. Blood thinners

70. When should a woman consider a hysterectomy?

a. When she is experiencing intense periods
b. When the uterus experiences a prolapse
c. When she has uterine cancer
d. All of the above

71. What is one fact about the fibroids in the woman's uterus?

a. They are noncancerous
b. They may be cancerous
c. They may cause punctures around the body
d. They may affect the woman's bowel movements

72. A Ringer's lactate solution may be administered when a patient:

a. Has experienced intense fatigue
b. Has hypotension
c. Has a slow heart rate
d. Needs to keep his or her blood sugar level balanced

73. Heliox is a mixture of helium and oxygen that relieves airway obstructions. What is the ideal mixture of helium and oxygen?

a. 80/20
b. 60/40
c. 40/60
d. 20/80

74. Can an expectorant work in the treatment of bronchitis?

a. As a first solution
b. Never
c. Only if other treatments do not work
d. Depends on how severe the case is

75. The innermost layer of the heart is the:
    a. Endocardium
    b. Pericardium
    c. Myocardium
    d. All of them are in the same area

76. Which of the following is a fact about ventricular fibrillation?
    a. Treatment is required immediately
    b. The patient should be observed to see if the condition can resolve itself
    c. The patient may require rest
    d. Each patient's treatment should be unique

77. What does it mean when red blood cells become packed?
    a. They are hydrated
    b. They are separated for a transfusion
    c. They have more white blood cells
    d. They have been sorted to ensure only one type of blood is in there

78. What is the greatest concern when it comes to a patient's white blood cell count?
    a. White blood cells attacking one another
    b. A white cell count dropping below 200
    c. An unusually high white cell count
    d. A patient losing white blood cells during a transfusion

79. A patient has been given the wrong medication for a treatment. The patient has dementia and does not understand the apology a medical professional offers. What should a nurse not do in this situation?
    a. Call a manager
    b. Talk with a student about always double-checking medications
    c. Hire someone else to explain the issue to the patient's family
    d. Avoid discussing the situation unless anything negative happens to the patient

80. A patient states that he has not gotten the pain medications that he needs during the day. What should be done to resolve the patient's issue?
    a. Commiserate on how other people have neglected the patient's needs
    b. Provide extra medication
    c. Tell anyone else responsible for caring for the patient how they have failed to help that person
    d. Ask a nursing manager what should be done next

81. A nurse is taking care of a celebrity's medical condition in a hospital. A news crew stops the nurse outside the hospital to ask about how that celebrity is doing. What should the nurse not say?

a. "No comment"
b. "I am not responsible for caring for the patient"
c. Any details about the patient's condition
d. State that the patient or the power of attorney held by the patient can provide information as necessary

82. An atrial flutter fires at least how many times in a minute?

a. 200
b. 250
c. 300
d. 350

83. What can trigger a thrombus?

a. Dents in a vein
b. Amniotic fluid
c. Blood sugar
d. All of the above

84. Is it acceptable for a nurse to give out medication information over the phone?

a. Yes, to anyone
b. Yes, but only to relatives
c. Yes, but only if the power of attorney applies
d. No, not in any situation

85. A person in a hospital slipped and fell on a wet floor. While a maintenance employee was told about the wet floor and a leak that was causing it, that person did not place a warning sign or marker in the area of the leak. What should be done here?

a. Review the factors that led to the issue
b. Figure out who is to blame
c. Review the hospital's hiring processes
d. Note the cause of the leak that caused the wet floor

86. What can be said about the Lantus mechanism?

a. The medication works in about eight hours
b. The medication works in about an hour
c. The treatment is short-acting
d. The treatment provides continuous medical support

87. What may be noted when a person with pneumonia coughs?

a. The cough is unproductive
b. The expectorant is discolored
c. The expectorant is runny
d. The cough is hoarse

88. Which of the following foreign bodies may be swallowed by an adult?

a. A dental appliance
b. Various foods
c. Bone fragments
d. All of the above

89. When should antibiotics be prescribed to patients with pneumonia?

a. Right away
b. After the airways are cleared out
c. If symptoms do not resolve in days
d. Avoid using at all times

90. A patient has experienced a substantial amount of dizziness and has also fainted recently. That person has not been using any medications. What should be assessed?

a. Blood sugar
b. Blood pressure
c. Body temperature
d. All of the above

91. A drop in blood pressure may be triggered by:

a. Medication use
b. Bleeding
c. An allergic reaction
d. All of the above

92. A lack of vitamin B12 in the body will result in:

a. Anemia
b. Hypoglycemia
c. Shock
d. Sepsis

94. A patient has a lung contusion. What could have caused the injury?
a. An inhalation injury
b. Chest trauma
c. Penetration
d. Any of the above

95. What kind of injury is a flail chest classified as?
a. Blunt
b. Puncture
c. Inhalation
d. Bruise

96. How high must a patient's systolic blood pressure be in order to be considered a hypertensive crisis? This is based on the mm Hg measurement.
a. 140
b. 160
c. 180
d. 200

97. Which of these blood pressure readings is the best a patient may have? This refers to the systolic and diastolic blood pressure totals in mm Hg for each.
a. 120/85
b. 115/90
c. 120/80
d. 125/75

98. When should a patient's spleen be removed?
a. As an elective option
b. If the patient is overweight
c. If the patient has a blood disease
d. Any of the above

99. What is the greatest risk that occurs when any bodily organ is enlarged?
a. Improper blood flow
b. Rupture
c. Fatigue
d. Hyperactivity

100. What medications should be administered to a person who has had his or her spleen removed?

a. Prophylactics
b. Antivirals
c. Immunosuppressants
d. Anticonvulsants

101. A peptic ulcer may be triggered by:

a. Blood sugar changes
b. Aspirin use
c. Fiber consumption
d. Gluten consumption

103. A protease inhibitor will block cells from taking in:

a. Blood
b. Glucose
c. Protein
d. Lactose

104. What is a sign of Kaposi's sarcoma?

a. Bleeding around the skin
b. Purple patches
c. The development of unusual moles
d. Certain areas are more likely to experience cuts

105. Who should receive the HPV virus?

a. Pregnant women
b. Seniors
c. Teenagers
d. People with compromised immune systems

106. How often should the influenza vaccine be administered to a patient?

a. Every year
b. Every other year
c. Twice a year
d. Once every 18 months

107. What organ should be tested prior to giving a cancer patient chemotherapy?

a. Heart
b. Lung
c. Liver
d. Kidney

108. What may be observed when a patient's platelet total drops?

a. That person will be more likely to experience bleeding issues
b. An infection could occur
c. A patient might develop temporary loss of some senses
d. Anemia can develop

109. A kidney stone of this size should be easy for a person to pass without medical intervention:

a. 4 mm
b. 6 mm
c. 8 mm
d. 10 mm

110. How long can it take for a kidney stone to pass on its own? This is based on an average-sized kidney stone around 5 mm in size.

a. 10 days
b. 20 days
c. 30 days
d. 40 days

111. A Pap smear collects cells from the:

a. Uterus
b. Cervix
c. Vagina
d. Rectum

112. Is a woman who underwent a hysterectomy still at risk of cancers in the cervix?

a. Yes, she is at risk
b. She is at risk for some cancers, but not all
c. The patient is at risk but does not need to worry
d. No, the hysterectomy eliminates the risk

113. What is the most important question to ask a patient who has experienced a great deal of weight loss?

a. What medications are you using?
b. How active are you?
c. What has your maximum weight been?
d. Are you trying to lose weight?

114. A patient with jaundiced eyes will:

a. Have yellowing in the whites
b. Have discolored pupils
c. Have dilated pupils
d. Not be capable of focusing

115. What can cause liver damage?

a. Fat
b. Alcohol consumption
c. Diabetes
d. All of the above

116. Vaccines are available for each form of hepatitis except:

a. A
b. B
c. C
d. All three of these have vaccines

117. What is a symptom of a vaginal yeast infection?

a. Irritation
b. Discharge
c. Itchiness
d. All of the above may be symptoms

118. A woman who has been a victim of rape or sexual assault should be advised not to:

a. Wash off until she has been examined
b. Report the rape or assault to the police
c. Take medication
d. All of these are fine to do

119. Blood clotting issues may be diagnosed using what test?
a. Coagulation test
b. White blood cell
c. Red blood cell
d. Plasma test

120. What should a healthy newborn baby's pulse be? This is based on the beats per minute measured shortly after the baby's birth.
a. 65
b. 85
c. 95
d. 105

121. What does the Apgar test state that a newborn baby should have after birth?
a. A pink look
b. Slight cyanosis
c. A few blue spots
d. A slow pulse

122. What does a biopsy during a diagnostic procedure entail?
a. Removing blood directly from the organ
b. Removing cells directly from the organ
c. A blood pressure assessment
d. Assessing the flow of blood in an area

123. When is an organ transplant necessary?
a. When a patient has late-stage cancer
b. When an organ is malfunctioning
c. When an organ has been punctured and will not heal
d. All of the above

124. Is it possible for cancer cells to be killed off by heating them?
a. Depends on the type of cancer cell
b. Depends on how many cells are involved
c. Yes, using an electric current
d. Applying heat can help in all cases

125. When is palliative care appropriate in the treatment of a serious medical issue?
   a. If other treatments have failed
   b. If the patient is at the end stage of treatment
   c. If the patient or power of attorney has dictated that this is appropriate
   d. All of the above

126. What is not a part of the FAST process for identifying a stroke?
   a. Face changes
   b. Arm movement
   c. Speech tissues
   d. Tingling sensation

127. A patient with cystic fibrosis will:
   a. Experience skin changes around the cheeks
   b. Experience nasal polyps
   c. Experience mouth sores
   d. Experience an increased likelihood of acne

128. A damaged pancreas will result in:
   a. Hypertension
   b. Diabetes
   c. Convulsions
   d. Seizures

129. What happens when a bile duct develops a block?
   a. Bile cannot move to the small intestine
   b. The gallbladder will leak bile
   c. The bile will go through the urine
   d. The bile will dissolve

130. What makes a hemorrhagic stroke different from an ischemic stroke?
   a. The hemorrhagic stroke develops from a clot
   b. An older person has a greater risk of developing a hemorrhagic stroke
   c. The hemorrhagic stroke is a result of a leak in a vessel
   d. The ischemic stroke occurs due to trauma from an outside injury

131. What occurs first during a migraine headache?
   a. Prodrome
   b. Aura
   c. Attack
   d. Post-drome

132. Which of the following can help a nurse determine if a patient has had a stroke?
a. Assessing how well the patient's arm moves
b. Assessing whether the arm is drooping to the side
c. Assessing whether the arm responds to reflexes
d. Assessing any visible changes in the skin

133. What could result due to bacterial meningitis?
a. Paralysis
b. Amputation
c. Seizures
d. Diabetes

134. Dementia may develop as neurological tissue experiences:
a. Physical damage
b. Blood pressure changes
c. Added connections
d. Disorganization

135. Is it possible for a patient to be cured of multiple sclerosis?
a. Full remission is possible
b. Remission occurs only sporadically
c. There is no cure
d. The condition can vary based on the situation

137. What happens during a tonic seizure?
a. Falling
b. Jerking actions
c. Facial spasms
d. All of these are concerns

138. Which of the following can be used to treat hydrocephaly?
a. Fine-needle aspiration
b. A shunt
c. A catheter
d. Antibiotics

139. A CT scan can be used to assess a spinal column injury. The CT scan can specifically be used to assess:

a. Discs
b. Inflammation
c. Nerves
d. Bone structure

140. A neurogenic shock in a spinal cord injury may cause:

a. Bradycardia
b. Hypertension
c. Constriction in the blood vessels
d. All of the above

141. What is the first thing to do when planning a blood transfusion?

a. Double-check the IV line
b. Test the donor's blood
c. Test the recipient's blood
d. Assess the patient's ability to handle the transfusion

142. Which of these antigens is not likely to appear in a blood sample?

a. A
b. B
c. O
d. AB

143. What is the correct procedure if a patient under observation misses a dose of a medication?

a. Skip that dose
b. Use double the amount next time
c. Consult a doctor
d. Adjust the schedule

144. A patient who has uneven heartbeats should be monitored based on:

a. Blood sugar
b. Blood pressure
c. How often the heart beats per minute
d. Weight

145. A patient with a low potassium level may experience:

a. Changes in heart rate
b. Excessive saliva
c. Lack of urination
d. A lack of focus

146. A vaccine has an attenuated form of a virus. This means that the virus inside the vaccine:

a. Is very strong
b. Is the reverse of the original
c. Is a weakened form
d. Is of the same intensity

147. The fasting blood sugar level in a patient is based on what the patient's blood sugar is if that person has not had anything to eat for:

a. An hour
b. Two hours
c. Four hours
d. Eight hours

148. What is an appropriate blood sugar total about two hours after a patient eats? This is based on the mg/dL measurement.

a. 130
b. 140
c. 150
d. 160

149. What antibodies does O blood have in its plasma?

a. A
b. B
c. A and B
d. None

150. What antigens does O blood have in its red blood cells?

a. A
b. B
c. A and B
d. None

Test 3 Answers

1. **c.** A feeding tube should be used. Anyone who is unable to swallow something should not be orally fed or there is a risk of aspiration.

2. **d.** The appendectomy may be performed with a laparoscope or through an open incision. Direct physical removal of the appendix is necessary.

3. **c.** The C2 segment is the closest to the skull. The C1 segment is the first, followed by C2 and then the thoracic, lumbar and thoracic segments.

4. **a.** Bulimia nervosa occurs when the patient compulsively consumes food and then vomits it. The condition may be triggered by anxiety.

5. **c.** Bipolar disorder may result in a person going from being happy to depressed in a short time.

6. **c.** The fragmental segment is not a part of the spinal column. The cervical, thoracic and lumbar segments appear in that order.

7. **a.** There is no specific reason why a person would be anxious. Generalized anxiety disorder does not require a specific trigger.

8. **d.** All of these factors can expose the bone to infection.

9. **b.** The legs are more likely to experience osteomyelitis than other parts of the body. The arms and spine are also at an elevated risk of experiencing significant damage.

10. **d.** The supine position is ideal for the patient. The supine position prevents cerebrospinal fluid from moving into the brain area.

11. **b.** Adenosine is recommended for the treatment of tachycardia. The medication regulates heart rate and will not cause any potentially harmful effects.

12. **c.** To avoid complications, a patient must avoid alcohol consumption when using morphine.

13. **a.** The abdominal muscles will be affected by the thoracic nerves. The other answers in this question refer to the cervical nerves.

14. **d.** The NANDA-I system is for assessing diagnostic efforts. The system helps to identify any possible conditions a patient has and any general pathologies involved.

15. **a.** A score of 35 means that a patient has a severe stroke. A higher Stroke Scale Score means the patient has a more significant or impactful stroke.

16. **c.** Digoxin is appropriate for the treatment of heart failure. The medication is an antiarrhythmic that restores the heart's natural rhythm.

17. **a.** Amiodarone is an antiarrhythmic drug that can help to resolve heart rhythm issues.

18. **a.** TPN does not involve the GI tract. A formula enters a vein that provides the body with the nutrients that it requires. This is for cases in which the patient is struggling to consume foods the usual way.

19. **d.** An orthopedic brace should be applied to control the position of the foot. An orthopedic boot may be of particular use when it comes to keeping the foot in a specific position required for healing.

20. **b.** A complete spinal cord injury involves a patient losing sensations in a specific segment. The loss of sensation in a complete injury will vary based on where in the spinal column the injury occurs. An incomplete injury would entail the patient retaining sensation in some parts of the body.

21. **d.** Osteopenia is also known as bone loss. The body is unable to create new bone and it can reabsorb the old bone structure.

22. **c.** The patient should add more calcium to his or her diet. Calcium is necessary for helping the body to restore itself and to prevent further injuries from developing. If administered appropriately, calcium also facilitates the growth of new bone tissue.

23. **d.** Pyelonephritis may develop due to pain in the costovertebral angle. The kidneys may develop an infection in this case.

24. **b.** Confusion will develop due to Reynold's pentad. A patient may develop a fever and a change in overall mental status.

25. **a.** Reynold's pentad is triggered by hypotension. The condition occurs due to shock in the body and can result in significant mental changes and responses.

26. **c.** Heparin is a blood thinner that prevents blood clots from forming. Therefore, it causes bleeding in patients. It may be carefully administered prior to surgery to reduce the risk of clots, but it must be monitored.

27. **b.** It is best to use Coumadin when there are multiple clots or thromboses.

28. **a.** The patient should avoid fatty foods during the recovery process. The patient should also avoid consuming excessive amounts of sugar.

29. **a.** Zofran, or ondansetron, is prescribed to prevent vomiting. It blocks the production of chemicals that may trigger vomiting.

30. **d.** A warm compress is suitable if a secondary infection occurs.

31. **d.** Permethrin should not be used in the treatment of cystic fibrosis. The other three choices focus on treating the symptoms associated with CF. CF does not have a cure, so the only treatment entails keeping the symptoms under control.

32. **d.** The Mantoux test helps diagnose tuberculosis via an intradermal tuberculin injection.

33. **d.** The India ink test uses a blood sample stained on a slide to identify harmful microorganisms that have entered the body.

35. **c.** The nurse should report on the threat in spite of confidentiality laws. The Health Insurance Portability and Accountability Act states that a patient who is threatening to commit suicide should be referred to the proper authorities. This is a case in which it is fine for the professional to share private information on the patient. The sharing helps ensure that the patient will receive the appropriate help.

36. **d.** The calorimetry measures how much heat is generated within the body. The heat may be based on chemical breakdowns based on the condition that the patient has. The measure may work in cases in which medications are to be used for treatment purposes.

37. **b.** The patient should not engage in fast-motion activities. These include things like driving a car or other fast-moving vehicle. There is a chance that the injury may become aggravated during such an action.

38. **b.** A score from 4 to 6 is an ideal HbA1c test score. The test is for identifying the quality of a patient's blood sugar. A lower score means hypoglycemia, while a higher one means hyperglycemia and a possible elevated risk for diabetes.

39. **d.** All of these factors will cause abdominal pain to worsen. Food consumption can irritate the body, while various physical activities can become extremely difficult to continue.

40. **b.** The patient will be diagnosed as having diabetes if he or she has a fasting blood glucose total over 126 mg/dL. A normal total should be under 100 mg/dL.

41. **c.** The person will be seen as being overweight. A patient with a BMI of 25 to 30 will be interpreted as being overweight. The patient will be identified as being obese if his or her BMI is higher than 30.

42. **b.** Lovenox is recommended for the treatment of a superficial vein thrombus. Lovenox assists in dissolving the thrombus and in keeping the area from clotting.

43. **a.** A lumbar puncture will not help in the treatment of thalassemia major. The other three treatments are suitable for use. Iron and folate treatments may also help, depending on the particular situation.

44. **b.** Cortisol is the key trigger for Cushing syndrome. A patient who is exposed to cortisol for too long may develop fat loss in the arms and legs, weight gain in the midsection and fatty deposits around the face and upper back.

45. **a.** Acromegaly develops due to excess HGH levels in the body. HGH is necessary for facilitating healthy growth, but an excess can be harmful and should be carefully monitored.

46. **d.** Hyperglycemia does not trigger Cushing syndrome. An overactive adrenal gland can be a cause, although a tumor may also be present on the gland. Steroid use can also cause some problems among patients.

47. **b.** Ativan should not be provided to the intoxicated patient. This is because Ativan works as a depressant and sedative, and it will worsen the depressant effects of alcohol, potentially causing a deadly reaction.

48. **d.** All of the foods listed here are good for treating acid reflux. Fennel and various other grains can also help. Green leafy vegetables are generally the best foods to recommend to anyone with GERD.

49. **a.** A warm compress will not improve a pneumothorax. The use of medications can relieve pain, while a chest tube may enhance lung function.

50. **b.** A tonometry is needed for measuring the intraocular pressure. The test assesses eye function, including whether glaucoma or other concerns are present.

51. **b.** Acidosis can be caused by a total parenteral nutrition routine. This is due to bicarbonate levels in the body dropping. Hyperglycemia may also develop in some cases.

52. **d.** The patient should consume less sodium. Since the condition causes fluid retention, lessening sodium consumption is key.

53. **a.** The Fowler's position is ideal for a patient with ascites. The position provides comfort to the upper part of the body and improves the flow of bodily fluids.

54. **c.** Morphine is appropriate for a patient with a CMO treatment requirement. The CMO standard requires a patient to be treated for comfort only. This is for cases in which the patient has a terminal illness and does not require additional intensive treatments. Morphine is ideal in this case, as it relieves severe pain.

55. **c.** Difficulties with urination should be closely monitored. A patient should not have problems urinating after surgery, although he or she may experience abdominal pain.

56. **c.** Any electrolytes lost should be replaced prior to the surgery. A bowel obstruction can produce vomiting in some patients.

57. **b.** A western blot test can help diagnose AIDS or HIV. The test separates blood proteins and identifies unique proteins that indicate an HIV infection. A further test will be necessary to identify the severity of the HIV infection and to determine whether the patient does indeed have AIDS.

58. **b.** ARDS, or acute respiratory distress syndrome, develops due to the shock and hypoperfusion that may occur alongside pancreatitis.

59. **c.** An HbA1c test is necessary for diagnosing cases of diabetes mellitus. The test measures blood sugar and how well insulin is being produced in the pancreas. A test may identify hyperglycemia and how well the body can handle its blood sugar stores. The HbA1c test can officially diagnose the condition and then confirm any

complications that have developed due to diabetes. The test may also be used to monitor how the patient is doing after the diagnosis and treatment.

60. **b.** Vitamin K can help with reducing the intensity of liver cancer symptoms. Vitamin K produces prothrombin, which helps improve blood clotting, thereby preventing excess bleeding.

61. **a.** Hashimoto's disease, wherein the thyroid does not produce enough hormones, is an autoimmune condition.

62. **d.** Hashimoto's disease cannot be cured, although the symptoms can be alleviated. An exogenous thyroid hormone medication can be prescribed for the patient. However, the medication must then be taken consistently in order to keep the disease under control.

63. **a.** An MRI should be performed to identify osteomyelitis. The MRI can identify an infection in the bone structure. Although an X-ray may also be used to identify a fracture, it will not necessarily find an infection.

64. **d.** Nothing is necessary in terms of medical intervention in this case. Since the Rhesus factor is the same in both the baby and the mother, there is no need to worry.

65. **a.** The patient's blood is A-. A patient who does not have the Rh factor has a negative blood measure. The patient would have A+ blood if that person's A blood had that Rh factor.

66. **b.** RhoGAM will suppress the pregnant mother's immune system. RhoGAM can be injected into the mother's body if there is a difference in the Rhesus factors between the mother and the unborn child. The injection stops the immune system from attacking the blood cells in the developing child.

67. **b.** A patient with trichomoniasis should abstain from sex. The illness can be spread through sexual contact. It can also cause an uncomfortable discharge from the sexual organs, not to mention it can make sexual intercourse painful.

68. **a.** The D5W solution would counteract any treatments for edema, as D5W is five percent dextrose in water. The compound removes water from circulation and moves it to the cells. This may be problematic for people with high intracranial pressure.

69. **d.** Blood thinners may not be appropriate for the treatment of uterine fibroids. Such medications can irritate fibroids and thereby cause the patient pain. The other three options in this question are all appropriate treatments that can lessen pain.

70. **d.** All of these concerns are ones that would require the patient to undergo a hysterectomy. However, such a procedure can take weeks to recover from, and the woman will no longer be able to bear children. As such, the procedure should be done only as a last resort or if a patient requests it.

71. **a.** Fibroids are noncancerous growths. These will not cause any long-term health threats, although they can cause intense pain and heavy periods.

72. **b.** Ringer's lactate can be prescribed for hypotension. The compound is a sodium lactate solution that replaces fluids and electrolytes in patients with hypotension or a low blood volume.

73. **a.** An 80/20 mixture between helium and oxygen is recommended. This is the most effective solution.

74. **c.** Expectorants are effective if other treatments for bronchitis do not work. Guaifenesin can be utilized. The medication is an expectorant that focuses primarily on people who have infections.

75. **a.** The endocardium is the innermost part of the heart muscle. The pericardium appears first, followed by the myocardium.

76. **a.** Immediate treatment is necessary for Vfib. The condition entails the heart beating inconsistently in various forms and wavelengths. This inconsistency can be harmful and potentially dangerous.

77. **b.** Packed red blood cells are cells that have been separated for a transfusion. The cells are for patients who have lost a significant amount of blood or those who have anemia that is producing significant symptoms.

78. **b.** The greatest concern is if the white blood cell count goes under 200 per microliter of blood. The drop means that the person has AIDS. This is the end stage of HIV, as it entails the immune system having been compromised to the point where the body cannot defend itself any longer.

79. **d.** The nurse should avoid not discussing the situation unless a negative event develops. The relationship between the nurse and patient states that the nurse

should disclose information to the patient. In some cases, another party may be responsible for conveying the information in a way that the patient or that person's family members can best understand.

80. **d.** A nursing manager should be consulted in this case. The manager can review the situation at hand and identify the appropriate answer for managing the problem and preventing it from becoming worse in the future. The patient should never be provided extra amounts of medication in the treatment, as the patient could be at risk of harm if more than what is needed is prescribed.

81. **c.** The nurse should not discuss the state the patient is in. The Health Insurance Portability and Accountability Act states that the nurse should not give out information on a patient's condition unless the patient says otherwise. The power of attorney may also be provided to another party who will allow the nurse to give out that information, but only under certain rules.

82. **b.** An atrial flutter entails the focus firing at least 250 times per minute. The total can go up to 350 times in a minute depending on the condition.

83. **b.** Amniotic fluid can cause the development of a thrombus. The fluid produces intense irritation in the body and can result in a clot. Any other outside fluid that enters the bloodstream may also trigger the concern.

84. **c.** Information can be given out over the phone if the power of attorney applies. The power of attorney should provide the nurse permission for doing so. This is the only case in which the nurse is legally allowed to provide health information to people over the phone.

85. **a.** The hospital should review the factors that led to the issue. This involves a root cause analysis to determine what prompted certain decisions to be made that would put the safety of people in the hospital in jeopardy.

86. **d.** The Lantus mechanism provides a long-term amount of support for the patient. The mechanism provides insulin to the patient for as long as necessary. This is for cases in which the patient's blood sugar level may be unstable and could be at risk of harm.

87. **b.** The cough secretions of a person with pneumonia may be discolored. This can be a sign of an infection or another issue.

88. **d.** All of these factors can cause a foreign body aspiration to develop in an adult. The aspiration can cause significant harm to the airway. In the case of bone fragments, this may come about due to a fracture or other break.

89. **c.** Antibiotics can be prescribed in this case only if symptoms do not resolve in days. The treatment of pneumonia should entail suctioning the airways and replacing electrolytes. Antibiotics will work when these issues have not been resolved as well as hoped.

90. **b.** Blood pressure should be noted in this case. A person who experiences a quick drop of about 20 to 30 mm Hg in blood pressure may potentially experience difficult symptoms.

91. **d.** All of these threats can get in the way of a patient's blood pressure. A drop in blood pressure can be produced due to the blood not responding well to an allergen or from medications potentially influencing blood flow.

92. **a.** Anemia results due to a lack of vitamin B12 in the body. The vitamin is critical for the formation of healthy red blood cells. When the body does not take in vitamin B12, it becomes easier for the blood to clot and for cells to become misshapen.

94. **b.** Chest trauma will be responsible for the contusion. The lung has a deep bruise, but it does not appear to be leaking anything like what would happen if a puncture wound had occurred.

95. **a.** A flail chest injury may be seen as a blunt injury. Blunt-force trauma can cause rib fractures.

96. **c.** Any case in which the systolic blood pressure is at least 180 mm Hg should be interpreted as a hypertensive event that must be treated immediately. Hypertension has already developed when the systolic pressure reaches 140 mm Hg or higher.

97. **c.** 120/80 is the best possible blood pressure among all these choices. Normal blood pressure should be 120/80 or less. The other three entries are cases of blood pressure in which only one part of the pressure is higher than what is acceptable.

98. **c.** The spleen can be removed if the patient has a blood disease. Other treatments should be performed first, as the patient will have a compromised immune system if the spleen is removed. But sometimes the spleen itself might impact the health of a

person's blood. In such cases, the patient will need to have the spleen surgically removed.

99. **b.** A rupture can develop when an organ becomes overly enlarged. The rupture may develop as the organ's tissues swell excessively and leak or burst.

100. **a.** Prophylactics should be used in a patient's daily routine if the spleen has been removed. Such medications are helpful for controlling the immune system and in ensuring it can fend off various physical concerns.

101. **b.** Aspirin use can produce a peptic ulcer. Other medications may potentially trigger the development of an ulcer, including SSRIs.

103. **c.** A protease inhibitor will block protein from entering a cell. The functionality will vary based on the medication, but it will identify proteins that might cause certain illnesses to develop and prevent them from impacting the body.

104. **b.** Purple patches can appear around the skin due to Kaposi's sarcoma.

105. **c.** Teenagers should receive the HPV vaccine. The vaccine will not work well for patients 26 years of age or older. Pregnant women should avoid the HPV vaccine, as it may cause harm to the unborn child.

106. **a.** The flu vaccine should be administered every year. This is to provide the patient with full protection over whatever version of the flu virus may be present in the coming season. Also, the effects of the flu vaccine will wear out a few months after it is first administered.

107. **c.** The liver should be tested before administering chemotherapy. The test identifies if the liver is capable of taking in the chemotherapy medication. Chemotherapy drugs are extremely strong and could potentially harm the body if the liver cannot process them correctly.

108. **a.** A person with a lowered amount of platelets will be more likely to experience bleeding issues. Such bleeding concerns will develop due to the platelets not helping to produce regular clotting functions within the body.

109. **a.** A patient with a 4 mm kidney stone should not struggle to pass it without medical intervention. However, the process of actually passing the stone may be painful. Proper treatment is recommended.

110. **c.** It can take about 30 days on average for a kidney stone to pass on its own. It may take time for the stone to stop forming before being excreted. The process of passing the stone may also be painful. Medications or other treatments may help with reducing the pain.

111. **b.** A Pap smear entails the removal of cells from the cervix. The cervical cells are then assessed for any evidence of cancerous growths.

112. **a.** The woman still has a risk of developing cancer. There may be a potential for some cancers to develop, although the greatest risk is removed during the treatment process. The woman should be monitored to ensure no new cancer cells develop.

113. **d.** A nurse should ask the patient if he or she is trying to lose weight. There is a potential that weight loss might occur even when that person is not actively trying to lose weight. Any sudden cases of weight loss without trying could be a sign of a more significant illness or other concern.

114. **a.** Jaundice can produce a yellowing in the whites of the eyes. The other features in the eyes will not change. The jaundice may develop due to the patient experiencing an iron-related issue.

115. **d.** All three of these concerns can result in substantial issues relating to the liver. Fat and alcohol consumption can weaken the organ, while diabetes can increase the potential for a patient to develop liver cancer.

116. **c.** Hepatitis C does not have a vaccine. Hepatitis D and E are not considered here, as hepatitis D exists only when the patient has hepatitis B. Hepatitis E is present only in underdeveloped countries and causes the same effects as hepatitis A.

117. **d.** All of these concerns can develop. A woman may experience a discharge, irritation in the area and itchiness in general. Redness and swelling can also occur in some of the most severe cases.

118. **a.** A woman who has been sexually assaulted or raped should avoid washing off. This is because any cuts or sexual secretions, such as semen, may help identify the perpetrator of the attack. They also may help identify the extent of the injury.

119. **a.** A coagulation test may be performed to assess how well blood is clotting.

120. **d.** 105 beats per minute is good for the newborn baby. The Apgar test states that a baby's pulse should be at least 100 beats per minute.

121. **a.** The newborn's body should appear pinkish. The baby should not have any cyanosis or blue spots. The pulse should be relatively strong at over 100 beats per minute.

122. **b.** A biopsy removes cells directly from the affected organ. The sample removed is very small and will not affect that organ's function.

123. **d.** All of these are appropriate times for an organ transplant. Other treatments should be used at the start before resorting to a transplant as a last resort.

124. **c.** Cancer cells can be killed off by heat via an electric current such as radiofrequency ablation. This process requires a few small incisions in the area where the cancer has developed.

125. **d.** All of the above times are cases in which palliative care can be utilized. Palliative care entails the patient being supported during the later stages of a medical issue when other treatments will not resolve the condition and the issue may be terminal. The power of attorney may dictate the use of palliative care in cases in which the patient is unable to respond to questions pertaining to the treatment process.

126. **d.** Tingling sensations are not a part of the Fast review. The T means Time, in that a patient will be at risk of significant harm if the stroke is not treated soon enough. The proper emergency medical authorities must be contacted to help resolve the issue before it can become life-threatening.

127. **b.** Nasal polyps are often found in patients with cystic fibrosis. Such growths occur due to the lining inside the nose developing inflammation.

128. **b.** Diabetes can be a concern for a patient who has a weak pancreas. The pancreas may not be able to produce insulin as necessary to support the body's normal functions.

129. **a.** Bile cannot move to the small intestine when a bile duct is blocked. The gallbladder will be unable to move the bile to the appropriate area in the body. This can cause significant harm if not treated.

130. **c.** A hemorrhagic stroke entails a vessel leaking. An ischemic stroke is due to a clot. The hemorrhagic stroke can occur at any age and can also develop due to fatigue or trauma to the brain tissue.

131. **a.** The prodrome stage is the first one to occur in a migraine headache. The aura, attack and post-drome stages occur after that. The prodrome stage can develop a few days before the actual migraine headache occurs.

132. **b.** The patient's arm may be drooping to the side during a stroke.

133. **b.** Amputation may be required due to bacterial meningitis because the bacteria attack certain nerves in the body, causing irreparable damage.

134. **a.** Physical damage to brain tissue can result in dementia. Dementia occurs due to brain tissue deteriorating over time. In most cases, dementia occurs naturally as the brain's cells stop working and the organ becomes damaged from general inactivity.

135. **b.** Remission occurs only for a short time. MS has symptoms that can appear and then disappear at varying times. In some cases, a patient who has MS will not show symptoms for months or years, but will eventually develop those issues once again.

137. **c.** Facial spasms can develop in a tonic seizure. The patient may also experience a loss of natural bowel control due to the seizure.

138. **b.** A shunt should be inserted into the head to relieve the condition, moving the fluid in the correct direction.

139. **a.** The discs in the spinal column may be evaluated in the CT scan.

140. **a.** Bradycardia may occur in a neurogenic shock event. Bradycardia develops when the spinal column receives an extensive amount of stress and pressure from an injury.

141. **c.** The recipient's blood must be tested at the start. The test will identify the patient's blood type, thus making it easier to figure out if the transfusion will work.

142. **d.** The AB is the least common of the antigens in blood samples. It may be difficult to provide a full transfusion in patients who have any type of AB blood due to its relative scarcity.

143. **a.** It would be best to skip the dose altogether. The patient will need to get back to the regular dosage schedule as soon as possible. The patient should never double the dosage due to the possible complications that may occur.

144. **b.** The patient's blood pressure should be noted at this point. The blood pressure may be dangerously high and must be treated as an emergency before complications can occur.

145. **a.** The patient will experience changes in heart rate due to a low potassium total, which can affect the heart's electrical signals.

146. **c.** An attenuated form of a virus is a weakened form of that virus. The treatment is effective provided that the patient has a strong enough immune system to handle the vaccination.

147. **d.** The patient should fast for eight hours before a fasting blood sugar test. This allows medical professionals to monitor trends in the patient's blood sugar levels.

148. **a.** The blood sugar total should be 130 mg/dL about two hours after eating. Any measurement that is under 140 mg/dL at this point is normal.

149. **c.** Type O blood features both A and B antibodies in its plasma. This is in comparison with type AB blood, which does not have either of those two.

150. **d.** Type O blood has no antigens in its red blood cells. The A, B and AB blood types have corresponding antigens in their red blood cells.

Conclusion

It is critical to be aware of what will be on the CMSRN exam if you wish to successfully complete the test. The exam will entail many things of value and can make a real difference when it comes to helping you understand your area of strengths and weakness as a nurse.

This guide will help you figure out the general structure of the exam, its main content areas, the time frame during which the test takes place and also provides test-taking tips and practice tests.

Good luck with your CMSRN exam. Be sure to refer to this guide often as you prepare. You will find that your ability to complete the CMSRN exam will be that much easier when you are thoroughly prepared for what will be on the test.

CPSIA information can be obtained
at www.ICGtesting.com
Printed in the USA
LVHW050217070720
659818LV00003B/61

9 781989 72614